The Artist Portrait Project

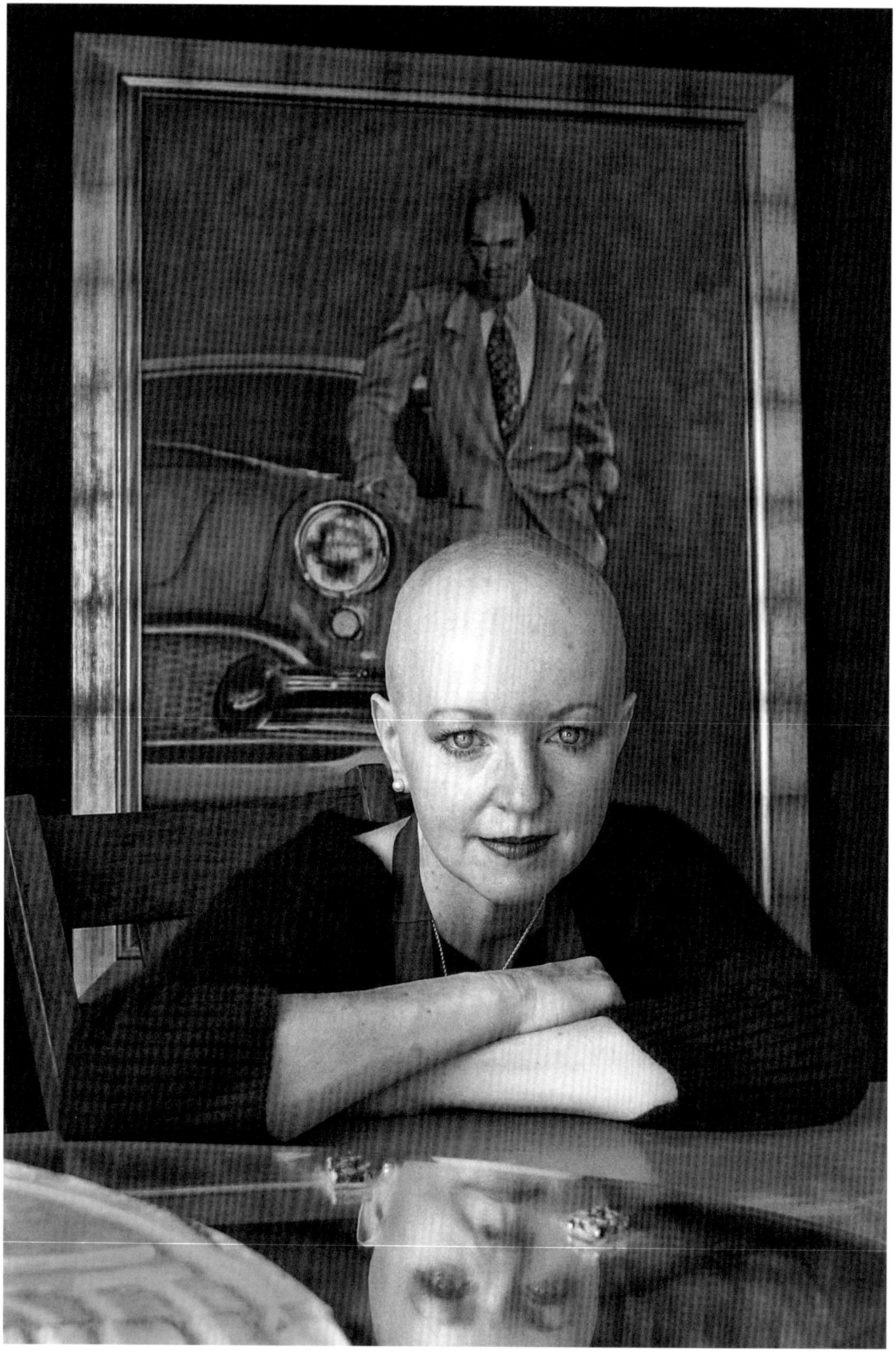

The Artist Portrait Project

A Photographic Memoir of
Portrait Sessions with San Diego Artists
2006-2016

Jennifer G. Spencer

SHE WRITES PRESS

Published 2018
Printed in Canada
ISBN: 978-1-63152-393-9 pbk
ISBN: 978-1-63152-394-6 ebk
Library of Congress Control Number: 2017964481

All photographs © Jennifer G. Spencer
Artwork on pages 8, 10, 46, and 112 © 123rf.com
Cover and interior design by Tabitha Lahr

For information, address:
She Writes Press
1563 Solano Ave #546
Berkeley, CA 94707

She Writes Press is a division of SparkPoint Studio, LLC.

To those who teach art and inspire others to create.

To Suda House—semi-retired professor of fine art, photography at Grossmont, Community College

Suda is a wonderful teacher who inspires her students to be creative with their work. Though demanding of her students, she is always supportive of a student's approach to subject matter and the student's learning process.

To Jim Noel—retired fine art photography instructor

With more photographic history and knowledge of film, film cameras, and photo chemistry than any other instructor around, it was a pleasure and privilege to learn from this master of the analog photographic processes.

"All photographs are memento mori. To take a photograph is to participate in another person's (or thing's) mortality, vulnerability, mutability. Precisely by slicing out this moment and freezing it, all photographs testify to time's relentless melt."

—SUSAN SONTAG

"Photography can only represent the present. Once photographed, the subject becomes part of the past."

—BERENICE ABBOTT

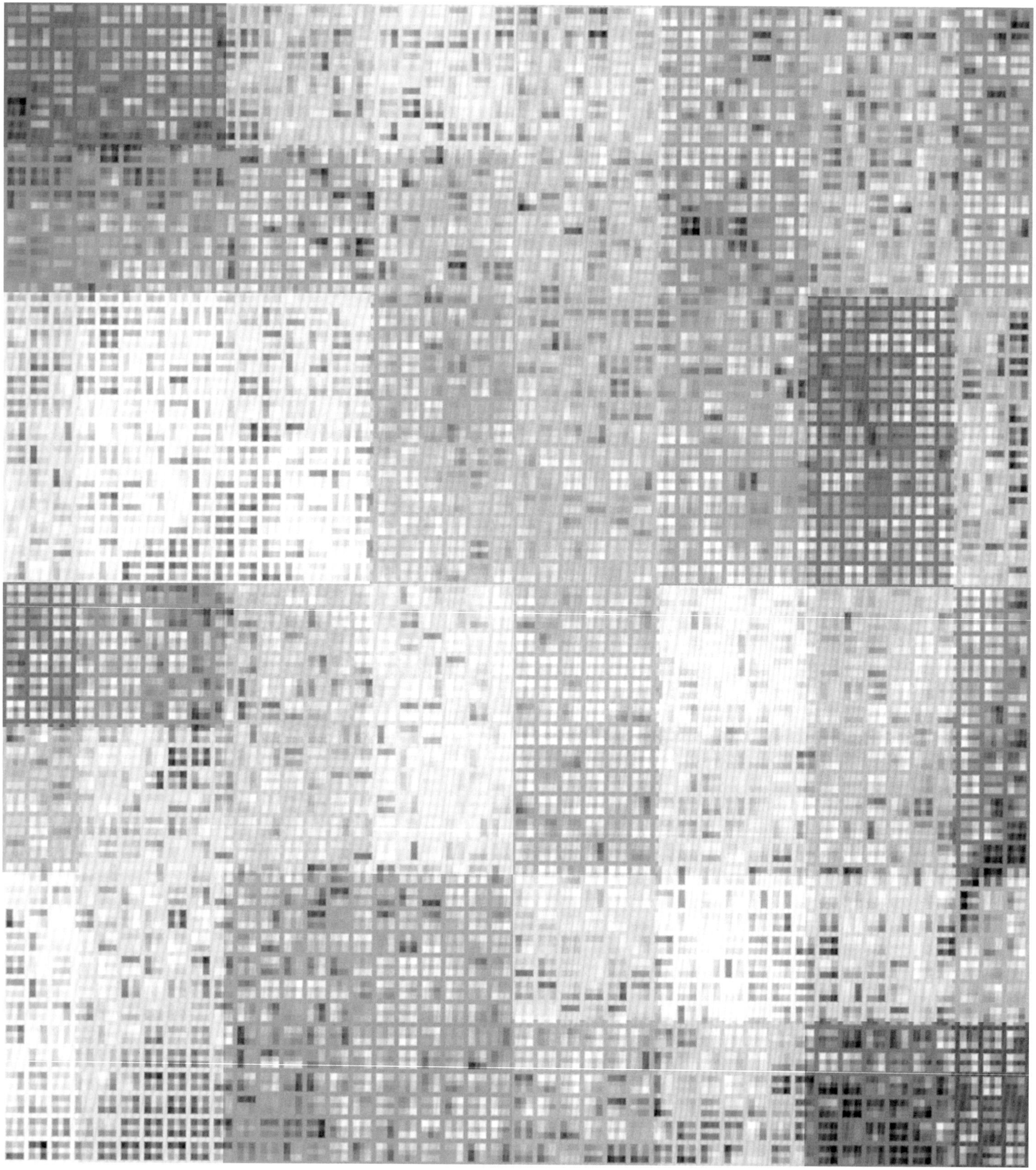

Contents

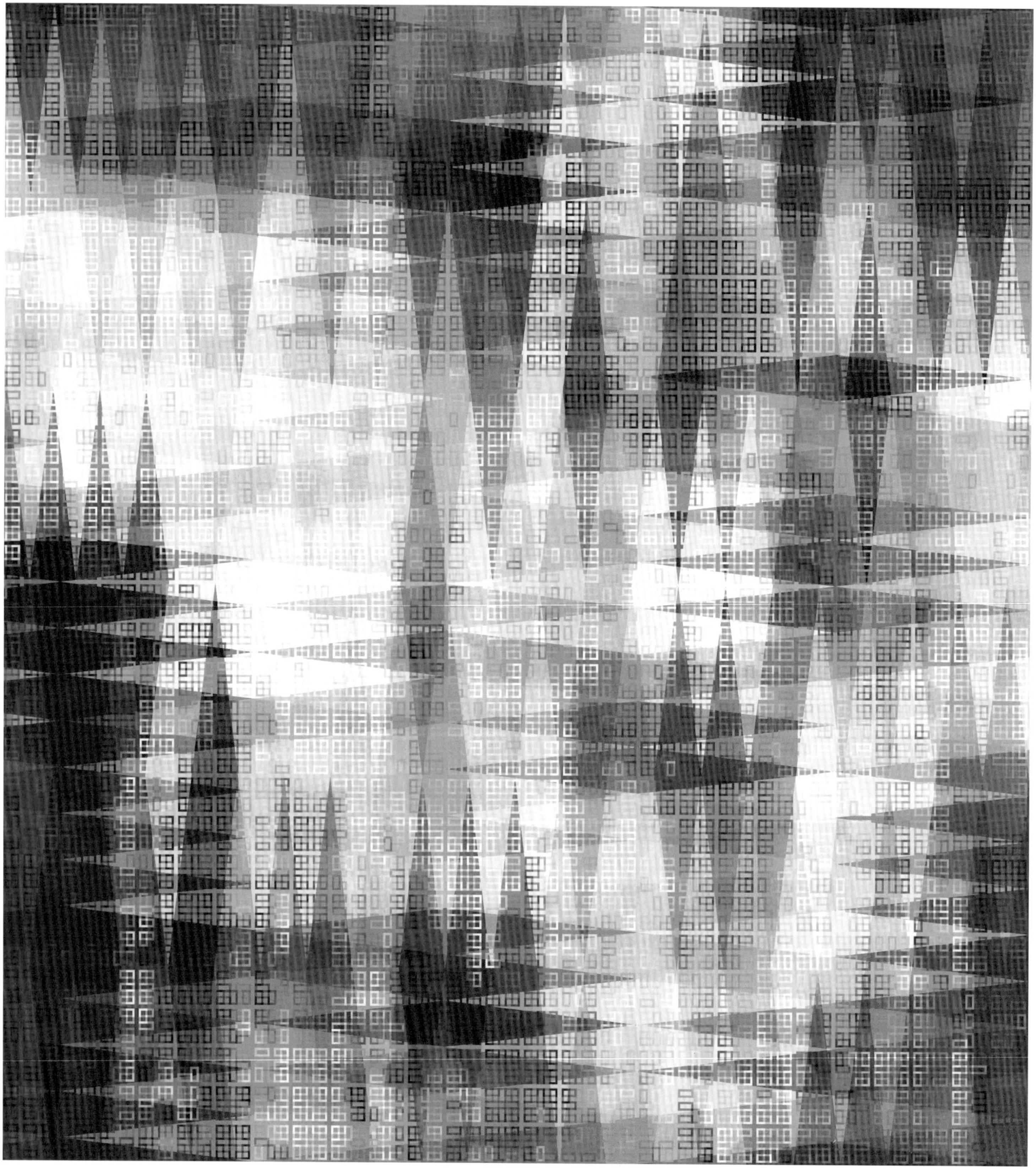

Foreword

The Poignancy of Portraits

Robert L. Pincus

Twenty-eight years ago, a local artist and publisher, the late Robert Perine, assembled a book called *San Diego Artists*. One feature of its pages was a photographic portrait of each artist selected for inclusion in a studio setting (there were fifty). Works of art have the capacity to remain perennially young, as critic Dave Hickey wisely observed in his essay "Air Guitar," but photographic portraits have a different effect. They fix our attention on the passage of time; they give it tangibility, a kind of quiet intensity. Berenice Abbott, one of the twentieth century's great photographers, expressed a similar sentiment when she remarked, "Photography can only represent the present. Once photographed, the subject becomes part of the past." To this insight, I would simply add that photographs become inextricably linked to our perception of the past. We think, for example, that most people in the nineteenth century were grimmer than us because they didn't smile in pictures; but we forget that for most of the 1800s the exposure time was too long to make that even possible. Such is the power of the camera-made image. It turns the past into visual icons.

Thus, the poignancy is palpable when we look at the pictures that Perine made in the late 1980s of artists who have endured and still thrive here, such as David Avalos, Anne Mudge, Jay Johnson, and Richard Allen Morris, while others have passed away, including Italo Scanga and Ernest Silva. Still others have moved on and no longer figure in the history of art here, like Gary Ghirardi and Gillian Theobald. But there is always room for another collective portrait of San Diego artists, and

I suspect Jennifer Spencer's series of portraits, which she calls *The Artist Portrait Project*, will also acquire a large measure of poignancy with the passage of time.

Spencer has devoted a sizable amount of effort to this project, which she began in 2006. It marked a departure from her foci as a painter and an arts administrator. And while she had photographed her own work for many years, Spencer had clearly decided to elevate her ambitions with the medium of photography. After retiring from her position as executive director of the Combined Organizations for the Visual Arts (COVA) in 2002, she undertook a course of study in photography at Grossmont College. Then, having given up her large studio downtown when Petco Park moved in, she decided to launch her portrait project and devote much of her time to it.

In her role at COVA, Spencer had developed a rapport with many artists. Several of these, along with other artists she has known and admired, have become the subjects of her portraits. There are fifty in this book and, while no cross section of this number can be called fully representative of the San Diego milieu, these portraits encompass a good deal of local aesthetic territory: painters, sculptors, and photographers. There are multiple generations of them, with an emphasis on accomplished figures who have been working here for three to four decades. As Spencer aptly writes in her statement, entitled "In Celebration of My Fellow San Diego Artists: Why Photograph Artists?", "This project is about the persistence of the creative spirit."

In my thirty years as an art critic in San Diego, I have happily written several times about some of those she has chosen. Anne Mudge, for example, whose likeness is doubled, as if to suggest the complex nature of her sensibility and sculptures; or Victor Ochoa, looking characteristically dignified, given his role as an anchor of the local Chicano art community for decades and as a multi-dimensional muralist and educator. Spencer's inviting portraits remind me that I have reviewed exhibitions or done interviews with many others she depicts: the late Walter Wojtyla, David Beck-Brown, Dana Montlack, Nilly Gill, Jeanne Dunn, John Abel, Becky Guttin, Cindy Zimmerman, and Kenneth Capps, among others. What Spencer manages to accomplish with these portraits is a keen sense of appreciation for each of these artists and a sensitivity to their different sensibilities. For Wojtyla, who had a penchant for fragmenting the figure, his portrait features something of the same effect: his seemingly disembodied head rising just above the frame of a painting that includes a head. For Montlack, whose photographic images delve deeply into the sea and its life forms, the setting is the seashore and not a studio. Here are three views of her photographing on the Windansea Beach in La Jolla, paying attention to tiny details beneath her feet, so to speak.

Viewing these images as a group, I can see that Spencer isn't trying to make some grand statement about San Diego artists, which is surely for the best. Spencer has simply crafted an appreciation, a personal chronicle of artists that matter to her. We can view and contemplate these portraits in the present tense, but they will likely have historical value as time passes. The meaning of the portraits is amplified by Spencer's written diary of her sessions, and its ambitions are outlined in her statement of purpose, "In Celebration of My Fellow Artists of San Diego: Why Photograph Artists?" People's memories will fade, but the pictures and Spencer's accompanying texts will endure as a sustained view of artists in our time in this city.

Robert L. Pincus was the art critic of *The San Diego Union* and *The San Diego Union-Tribune* for twenty-five years. He has a PhD from the University of Southern California and worked as an art critic for the *Los Angeles Times* before coming to San Diego. He currently teaches at the University of San Diego and California State University, Long Beach, and writes on art, books, and cultural history for many publications, including *The Wall Street Journal* and "Artbound".

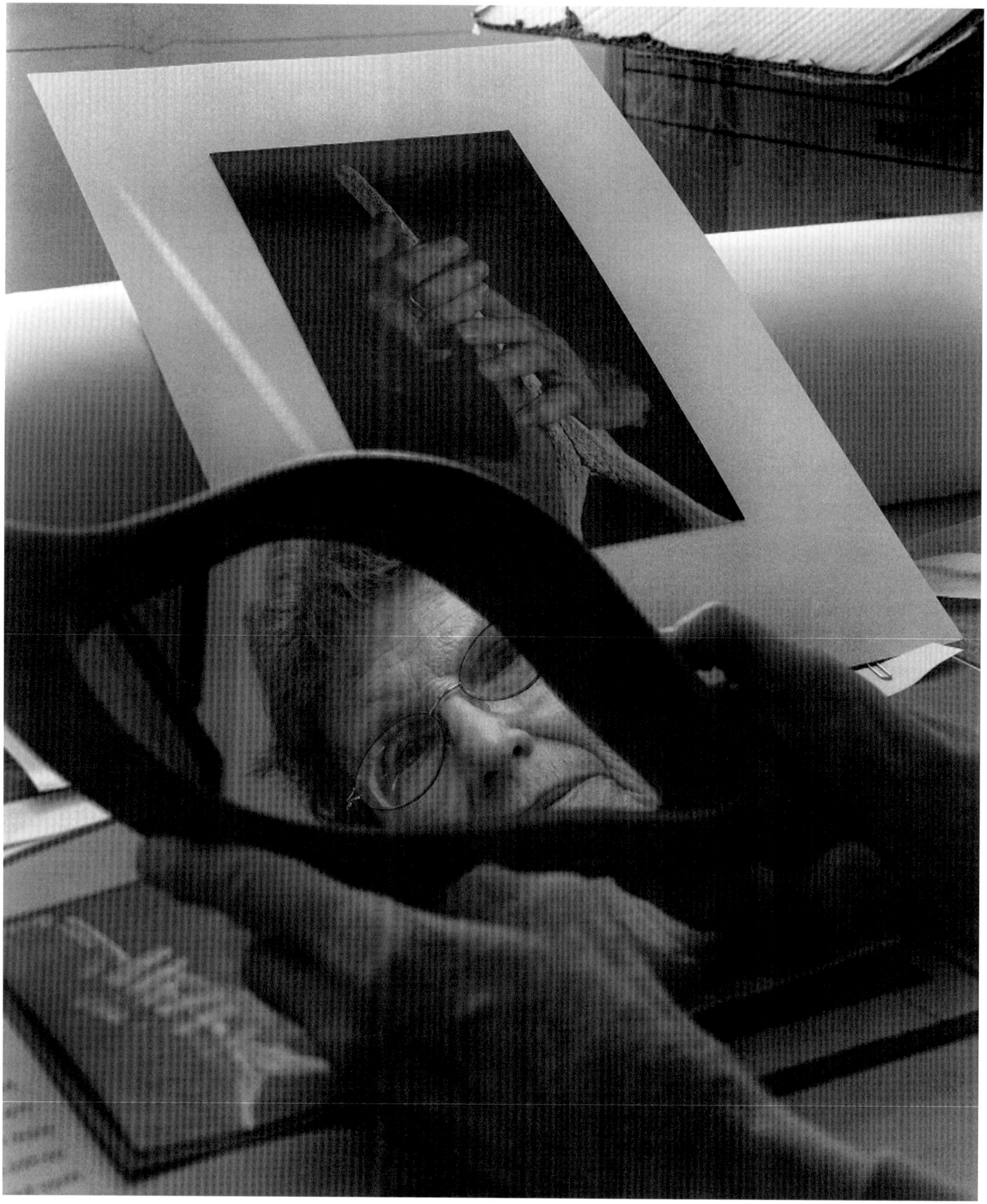

Portrait Diary

Comments on the portrait sessions, capturing "one moment of reality," Edward Steichen

Ellen Phillips

October, 2006

My first artist portrait subject has also been a long-time friend. Though my objective was to see artists as I know them in their creative spaces, it was more of a challenge in this case. Because I've known Ellen for so long, trying to "see" her was fraught with lots of preconceived ideas about how I should portray her. Ellen and Bill, her husband, are intrepid world travelers. Ellen's interest has focused on the cultures in other countries, their traditions and traditional wear, their fabrics and art. Ellen, who is known for her sculptures and metal fiber works, has been influenced by her travels. It became evident that I needed to reflect this part of Ellen that so influences her work.

Dottie Korn-Davis

October, 2006

My second artist that I approached for this project and good friend, Dottie, was a surprise. I'd never been in her studio before. She and her husband, Jeff, are also world travelers. Here is another artist whose work demonstrates how much other cultures have informed her work. An artist who's always physically moving, it was a challenge to capture her with her work in a way that expressed who she is. In the end, I used the artifice of shooting into a mirror on her studio floor, showing how fleeting Dottie is, with her paintings in the background adding an abstract element found in much of her work.

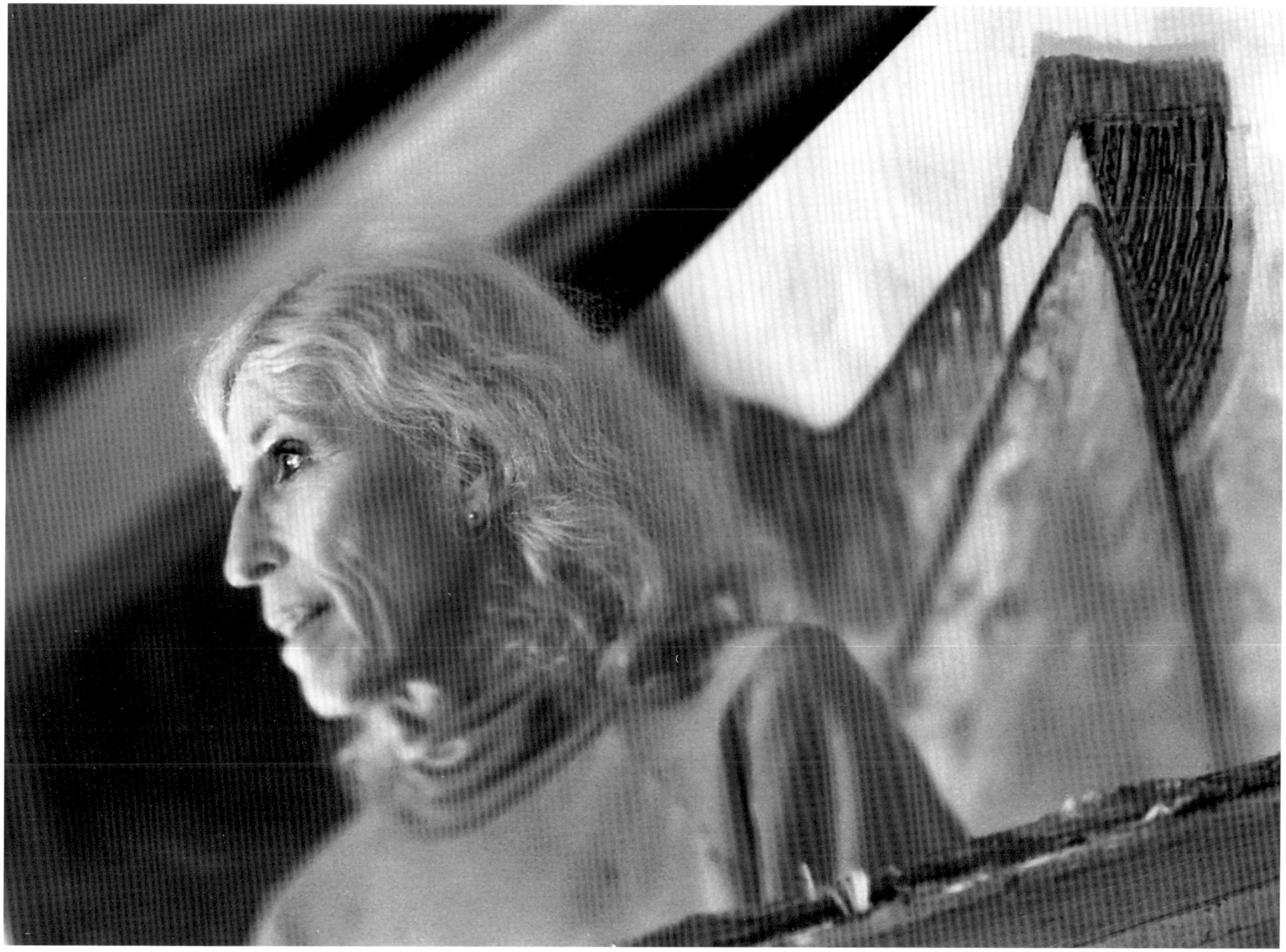

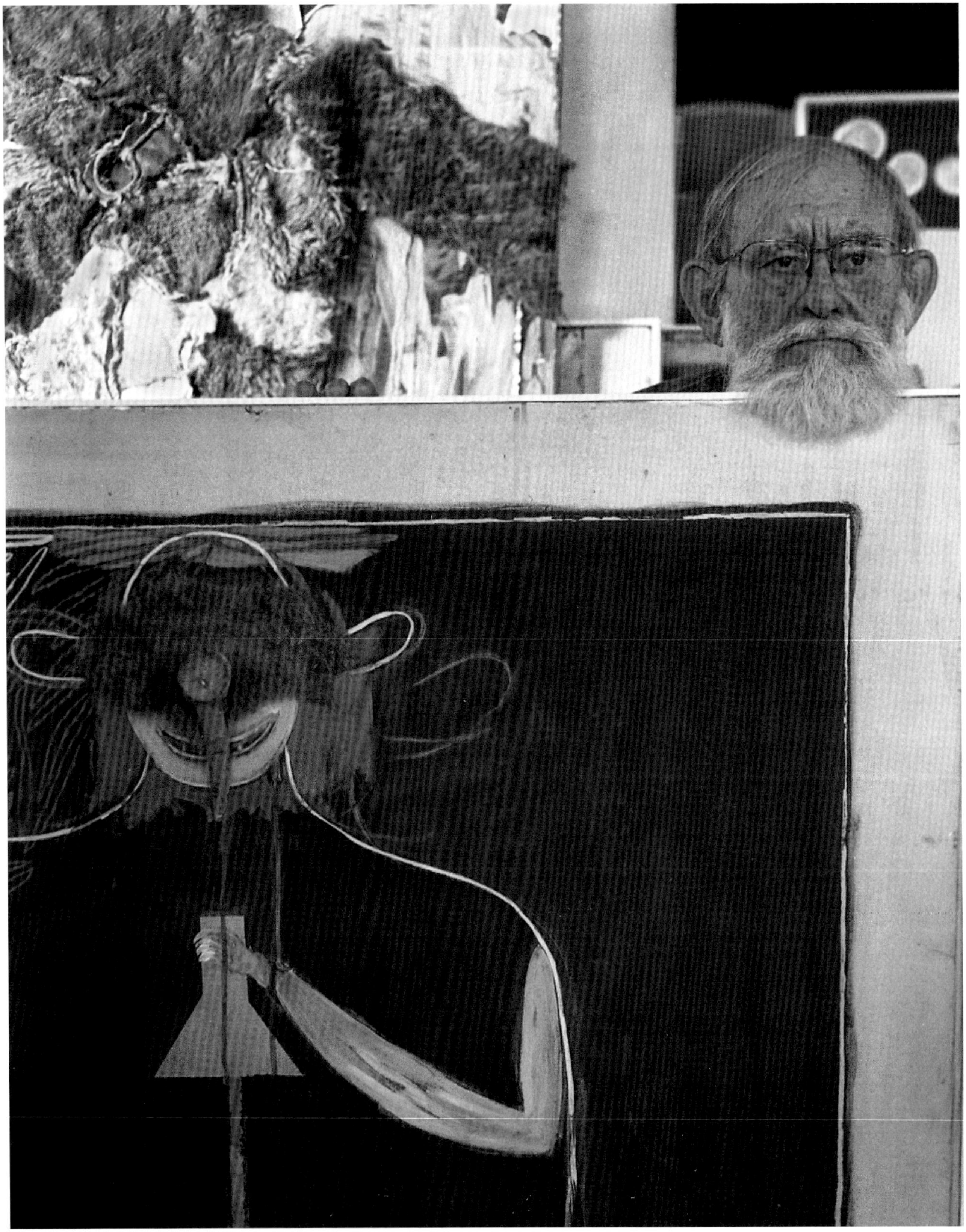

Walter Wojtyla

November, 2006 (Deceased December 3, 2014)

I'd never been to Walt's studio, but had heard it was packed with art. Initially Walt appeared physically lost in the space, so many large paintings propped up on each other with only a small path to navigate around the studio. It was definitely a challenge setting up my photo equipment. Walter always liked to play a character in some kind of comedy and was even taped for a show on KPBS promoting the arts in San Diego. It was his wonderful sense of humor and playfulness that made it fun to get him to pose amongst his work. His shower paintings portray women somewhat disjointed or dismembered, reflecting his love of murder mysteries.

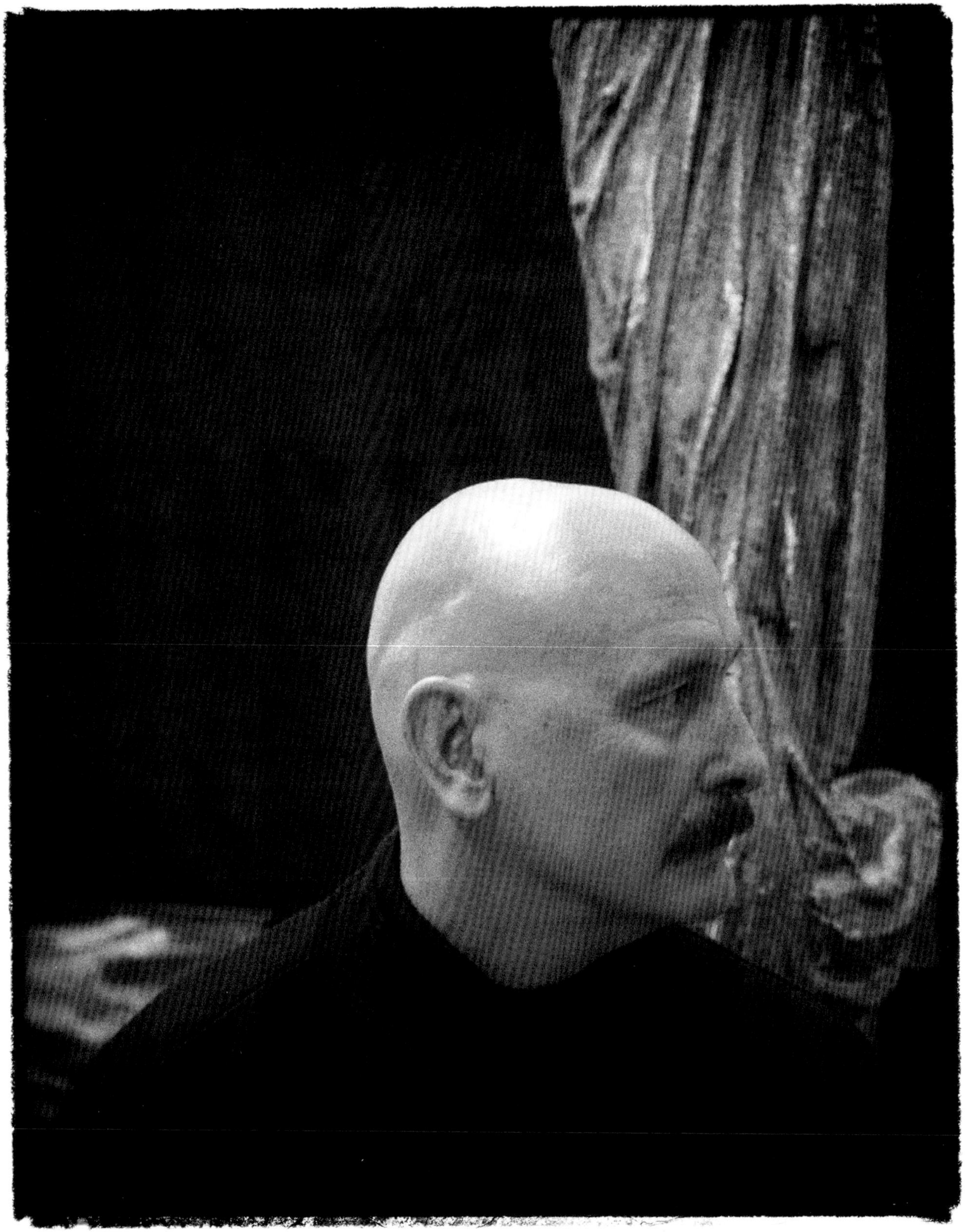

David Beck-Brown

November, 2006

I was not expecting to find a couple of bald artists, but David warned me that he would be "different." Indeed, he was . . . as was his studio mate, Kim Knox. Kim had recently discovered she had cancer and, due to cancer treatments, had lost most of her hair. As a result, Kim had her head shaved. In sympathy (I'm assuming) David shaved his head as well. I didn't ask. Individually, and together, they made intriguing portrait studies. David, who had been taking acting classes in LA played his role well. For this reason he was keen to have a portrait made. I felt portraying him in "film noir" format expressed who he was. The portrait of them together is one of my favorites.

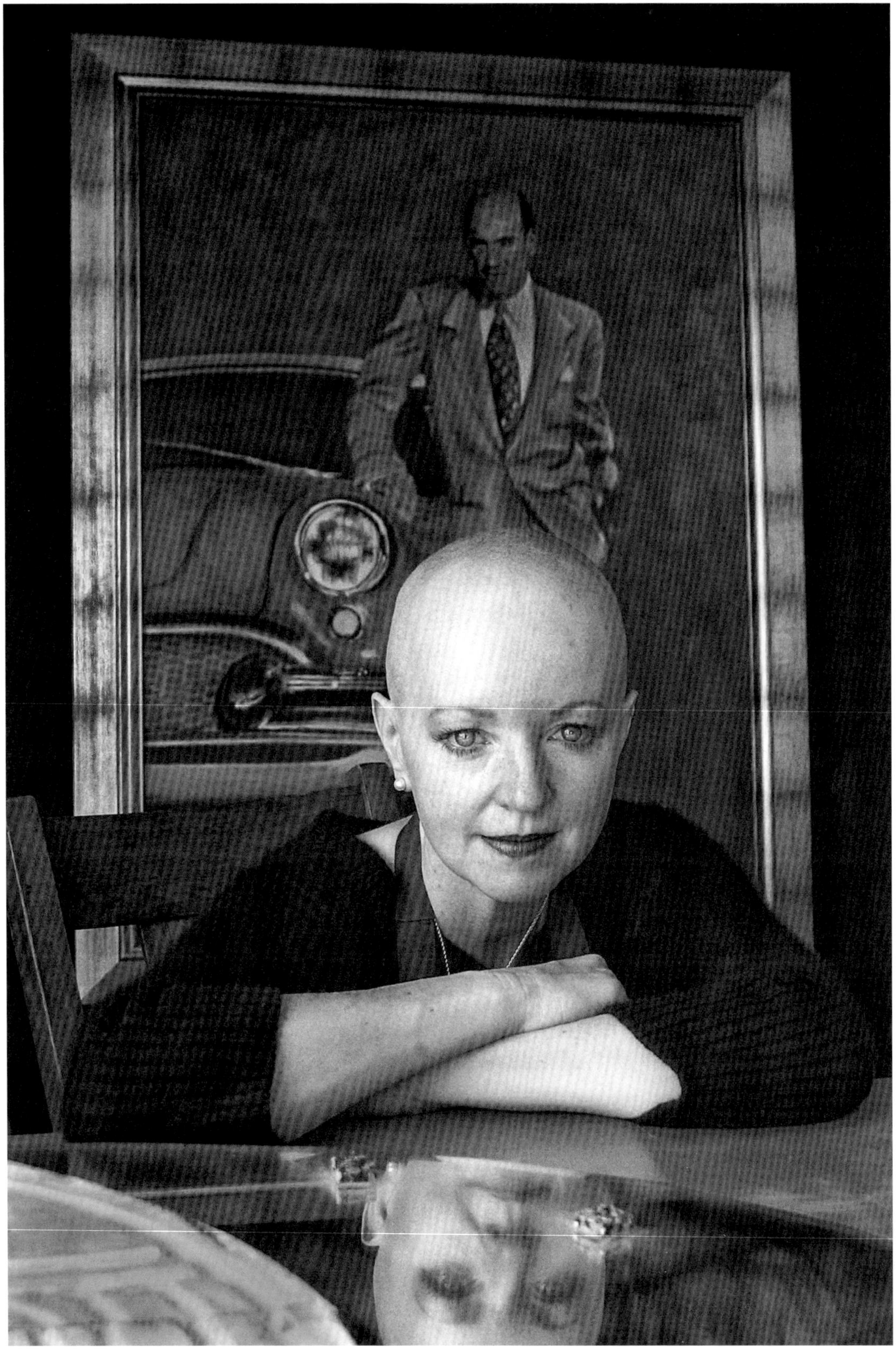

Kim Knox

January, 2007

Though I didn't know Kim, a painter, I was intrigued by how she looked without her hair. She had a beautifully shaped head that contrasted with her clear blue, water-colored eyes. As tired as she was, Kim was game to pose for a portrait with David. I returned later to photograph just Kim in her studio. I sensed she was in a different mood and not as tired as before. However, finding a comfortable place for a pose was still a challenge. We finally settled on a place near one of her paintings. Again, I used the artifice of a mirror to get her to look directly into the camera. I wanted to highlight her clear blue, water-colored eyes.

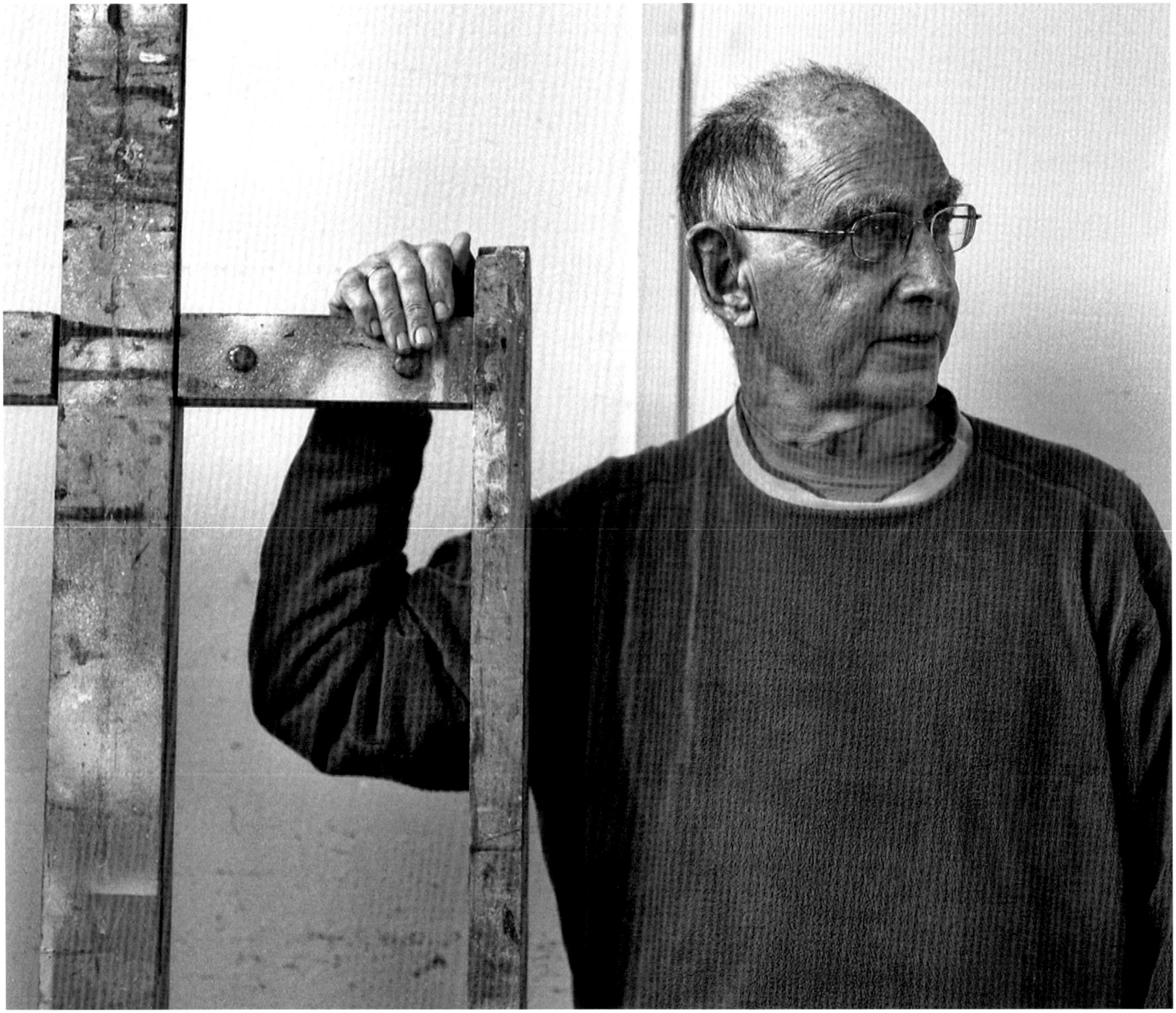

Carl Provder

February, 2007

Carl Provder, a consummate artist, teacher, and prolific painter, has influenced many painters with his mixed media abstract paintings. Another artist I've known for a long time, I'd only been to his studio in Encinitas once before, during Open Studios. The studio is large, airy with lots of northern light, Carl is as comfortable in his skin as he is in his studio, where he also teaches classes.

Jeffery Laudenslager

February, 2007

Previous to this portrait visit, I'd never been in his fabrication studio in South Bay, just his home studio during an Open Studios visit. In tight quarters with limited light, a large sculpture he was working on with an assistant took up most of the space. Hence, it became evident that Jeffery should be inside his new sculpture. This fit Jeffery's take-command personality and played this up as "master and commander" of his own sculpture.

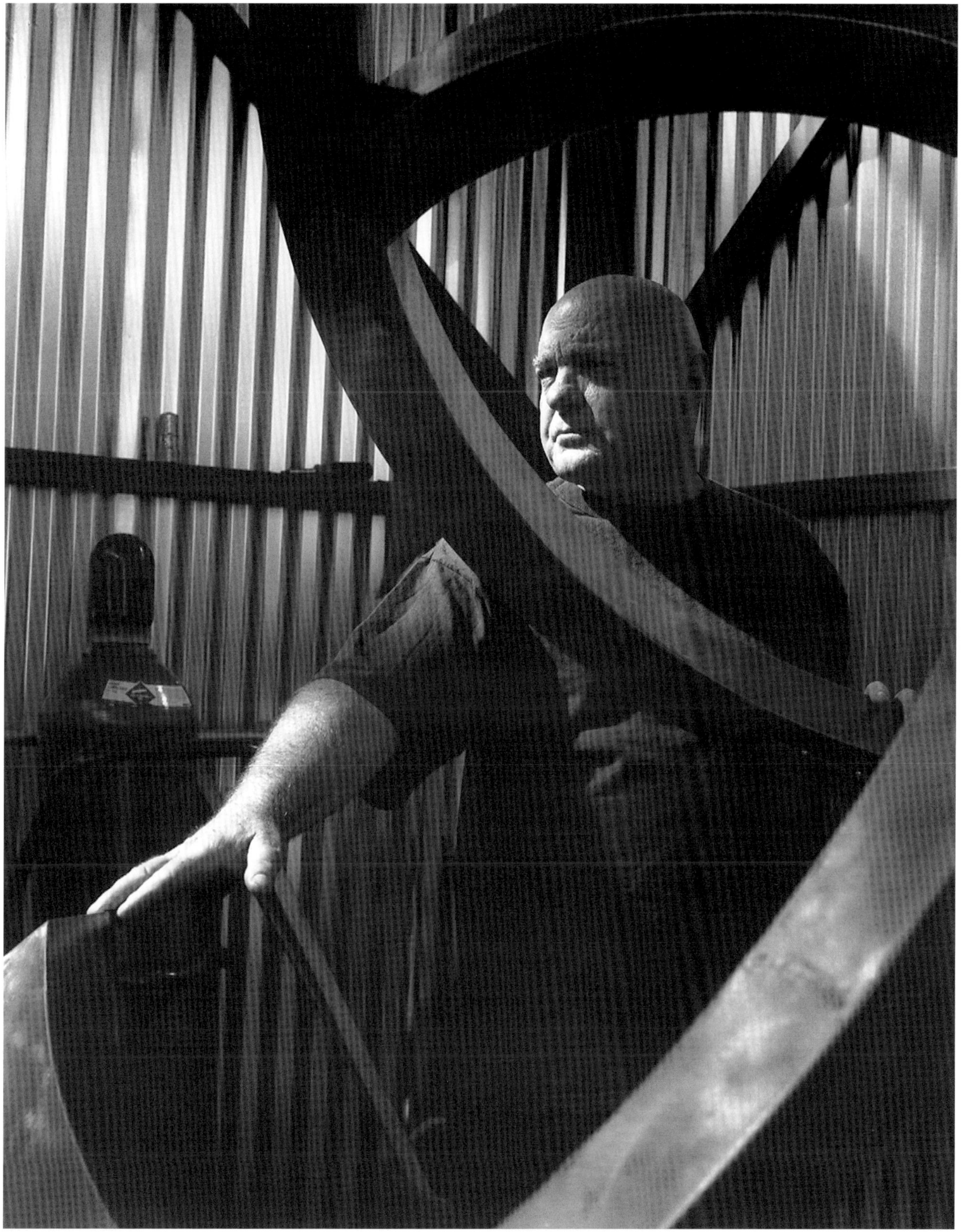

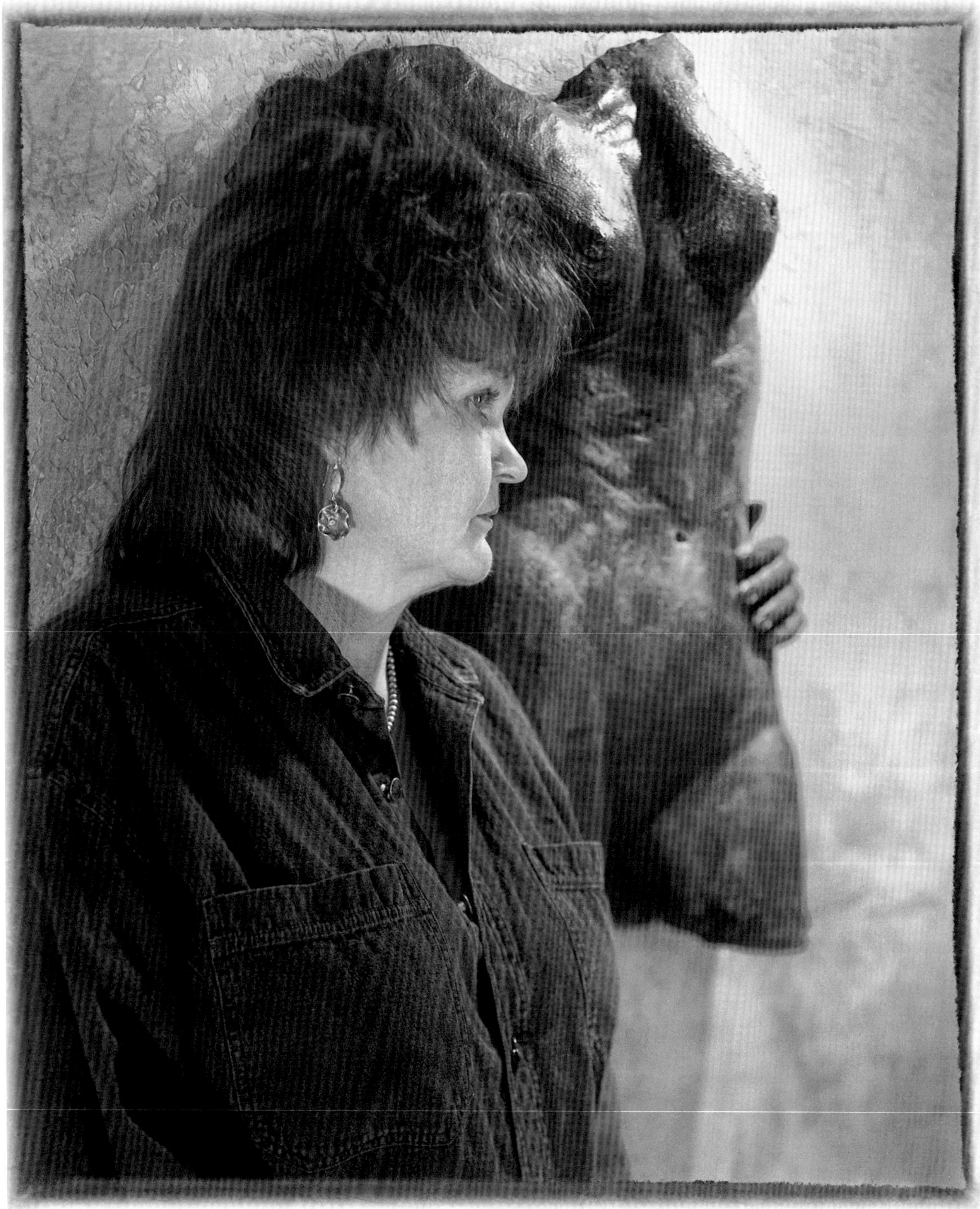

Leena Hannonen

March, 2007

A resident artist and graphic designer in Julian, I'd had the opportunity to work with Leena on Open Studios. Hard working and dedicated to promoting the arts of the Julian area, I wanted to photograph Leena on her land . . . outdoors. But, her inside studio environment was more conducive in revealing more about Leena and her talents in various art forms, including clothing, jewelry, painting, and sculpture.

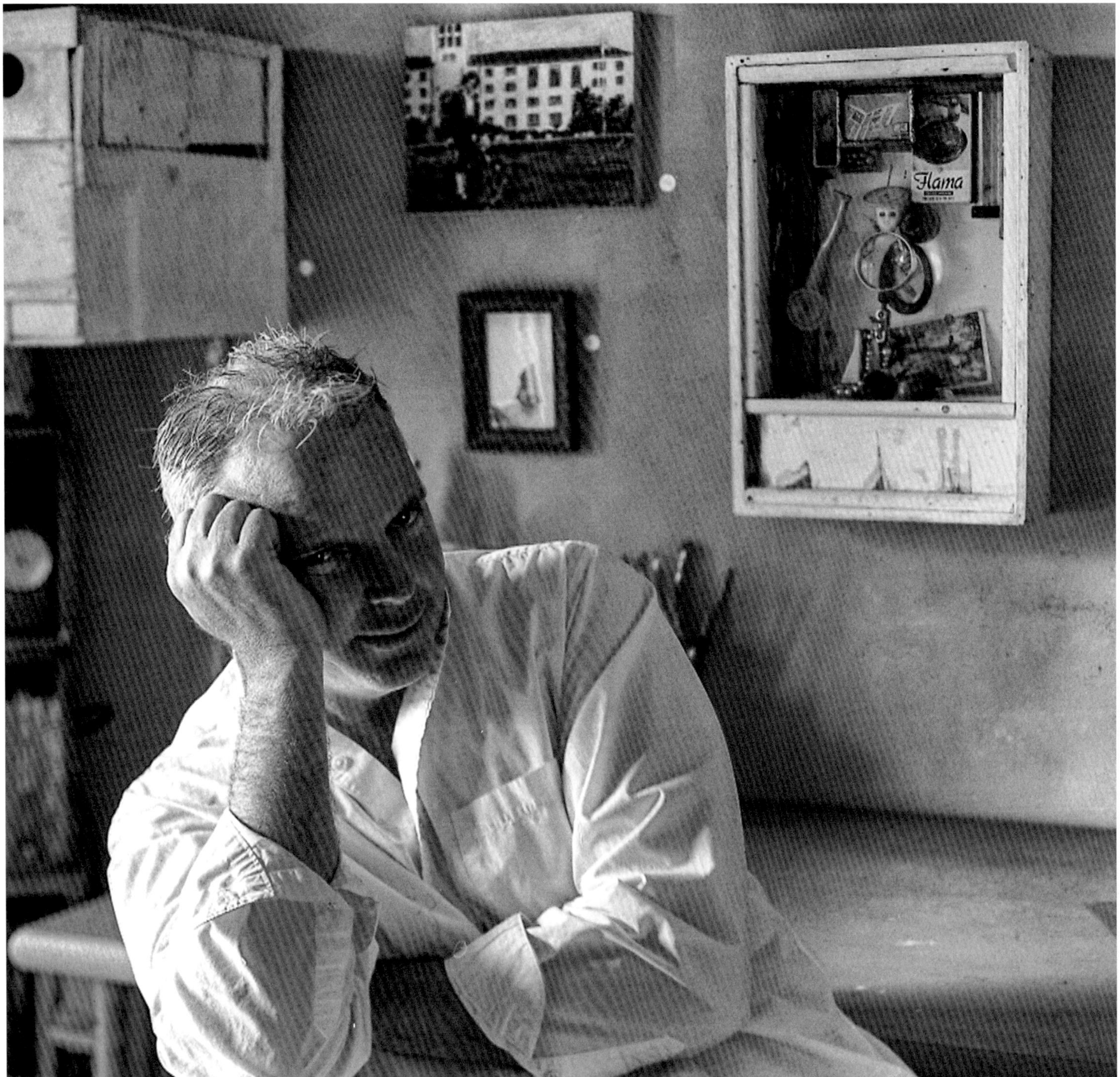
Flama

Joseph Bennett

March, 2007

Joseph, an artist of found object assemblage, injects humor and mystery into his creations. A bit of a free spirit, it was fun to place him in various situations in his small home studio, reflecting who he was at that moment in relation to his art. At first, he wanted to try some unconventional poses, until I explained to him that I wasn't looking for a pose. He has a theatrical personality that I'd not seen before. Finally, we settled in a corner with his work in the background. With a devilish glint in his eyes, I captured his playful nature. He and his partner now live in San Miguel de Allende, Mexico.

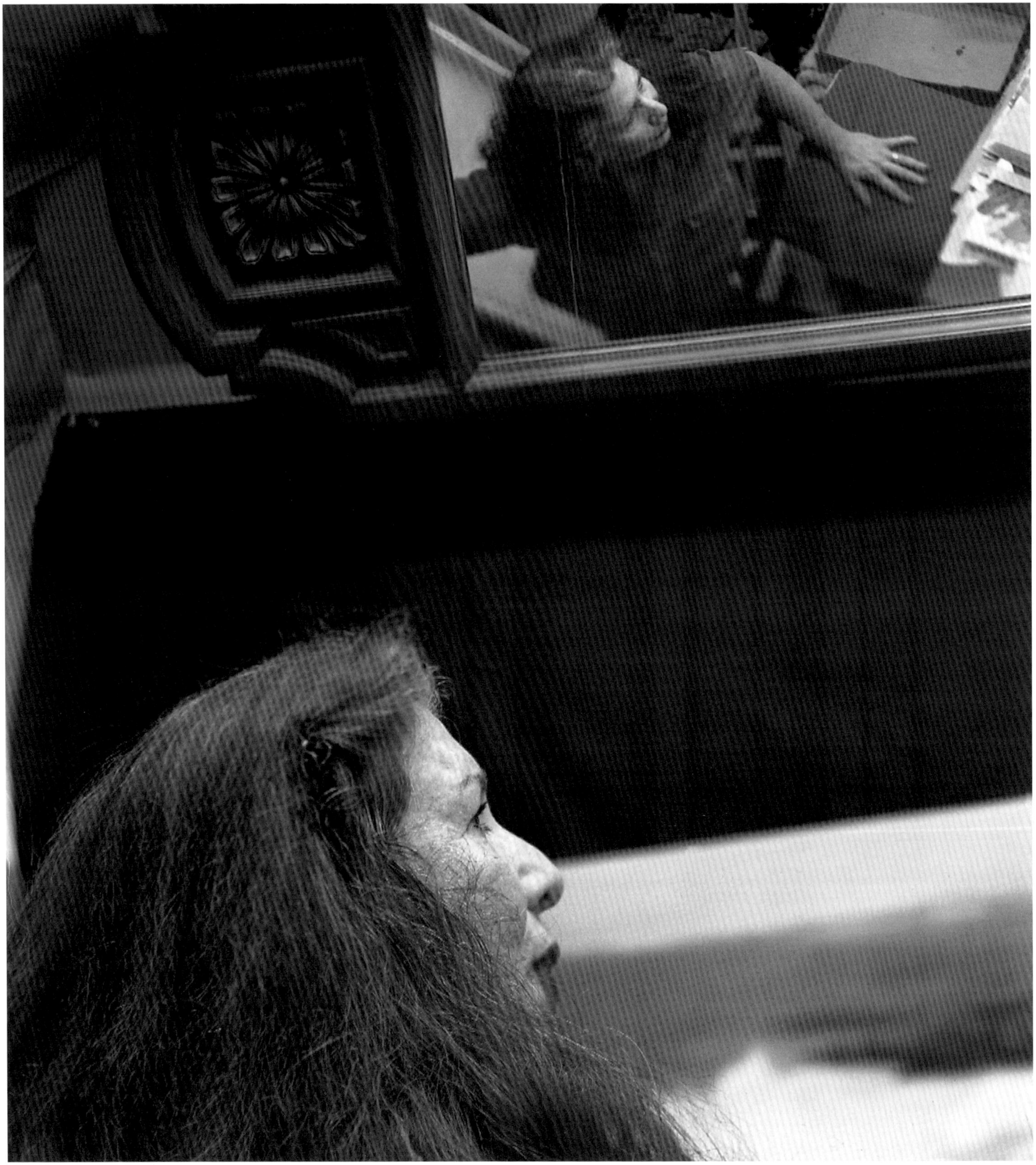

Nilly Gill

May, 2007

I've known Nilly for so many years, since the Spectrum Gallery in downtown San Diego. When I photographed Nilly, I didn't realize how much of a gardener she was until I saw her wild and wonderful backyard with a pond. Her studio is nestled amongst the plants. Stepping into the studio was like stepping into a different world. Nilly's unique painting style is reflected in how she set up her studio. Many painters use mirrors for various reasons. I was fascinated with seeing Nilly reflected in her suspended mirror and wondered about the settings for her paintings reflected by the colored drapery. Many of her settings are like settings for some drama to be played out.

James T. Hubbell

May, 2007

Sometimes it's challenging creating a portrait of such a multi-dimensional artist. Which side of Jim should I portray? His sculpture side, his public art side, his drawing and design side? The one thing that struck me about photos I'd seen of Jim was that they were all taken from a distance, placing him in some nook or cranny so that you would visually discover him by accident. What caught my attention most about Jim is how he artistically expresses himself, not just with the finished product but with his forward-thinking ideas and plans. Capturing him in a close-up looking forward, like a sea captain aboard a ship looking toward land, appealed to me as the way to portray Jim. "Sea Captain" Jim anchors himself in communities here and in Mexico, where he sees art as a way to improve lives.

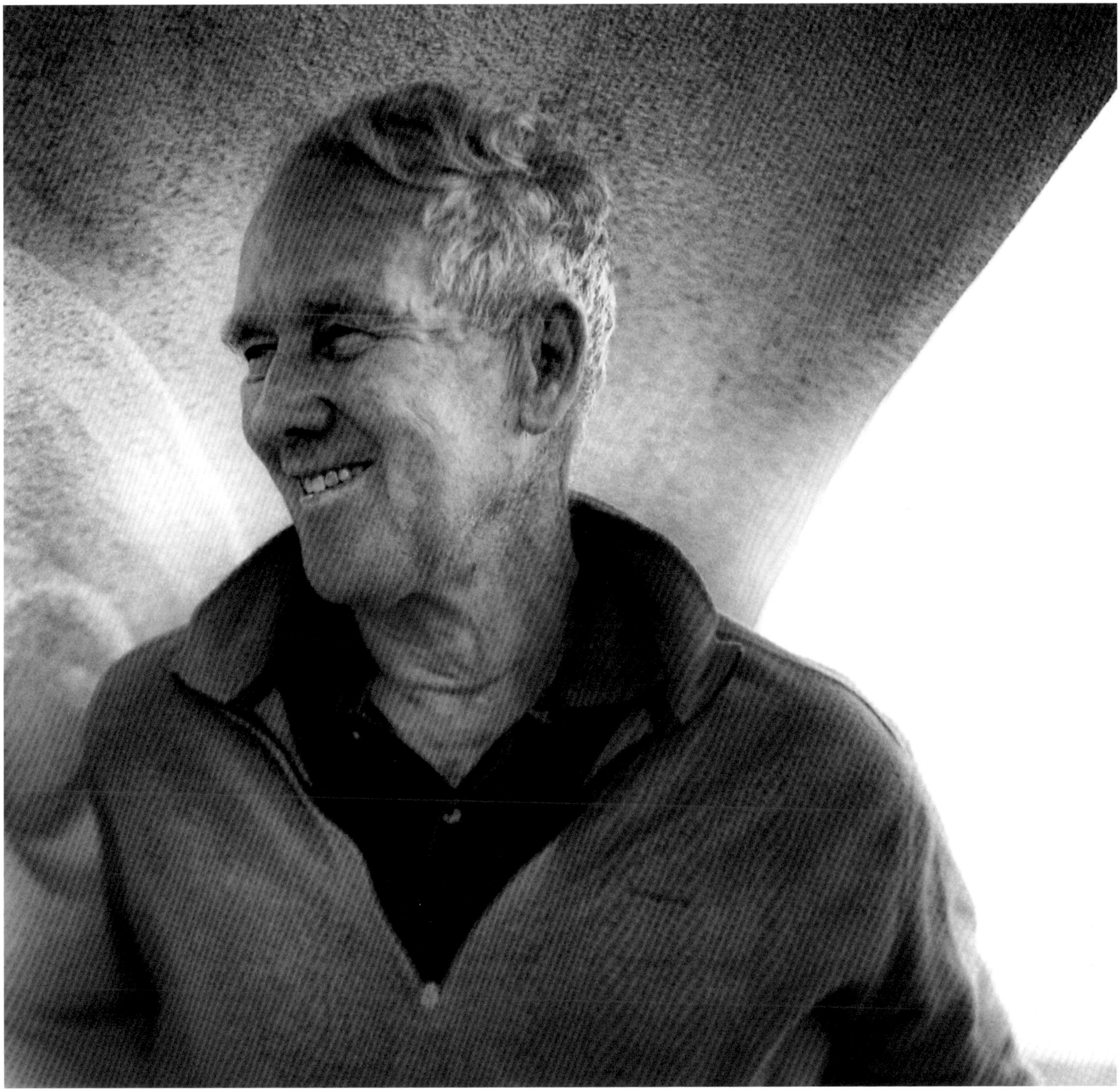

Deanne Sabeck

June, 2007

Deanne is an artist who works with light, creating beautiful meditative sculptures that capture and move light, using dichroic glass. Her studio uses natural lighting to highlight the sculptural aspect of her pieces while other lights help to create the refracted light patterns on the wall. As I stepped into her studio, the sculptures were not immediately evident until overhead lights were turned on. Due to the lighting situation, I really had to struggle with capturing Deanne's intensity contrasted with the more ethereal movement of light. Now, when someone mentions light waves, I think of Deanne's work.

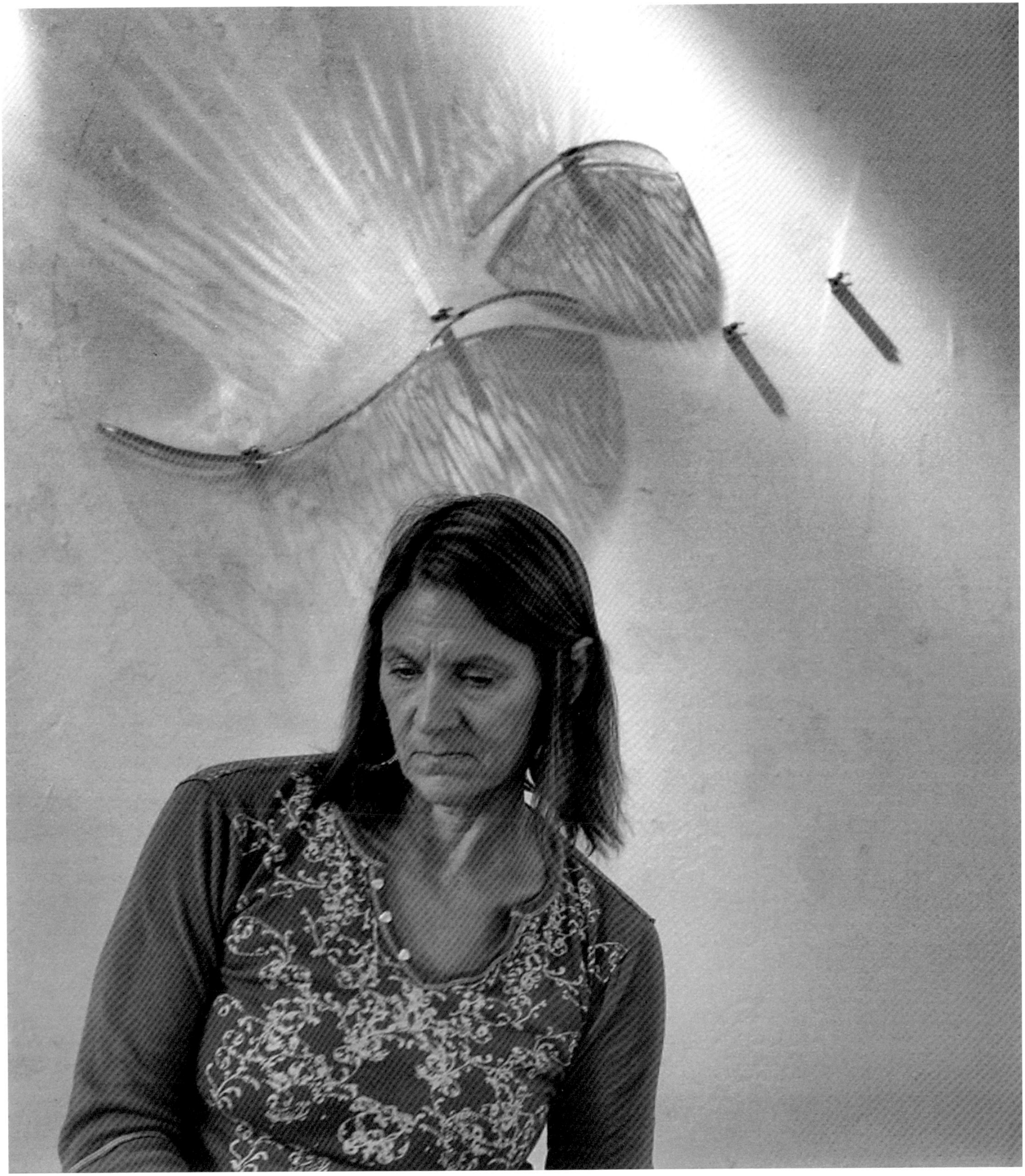

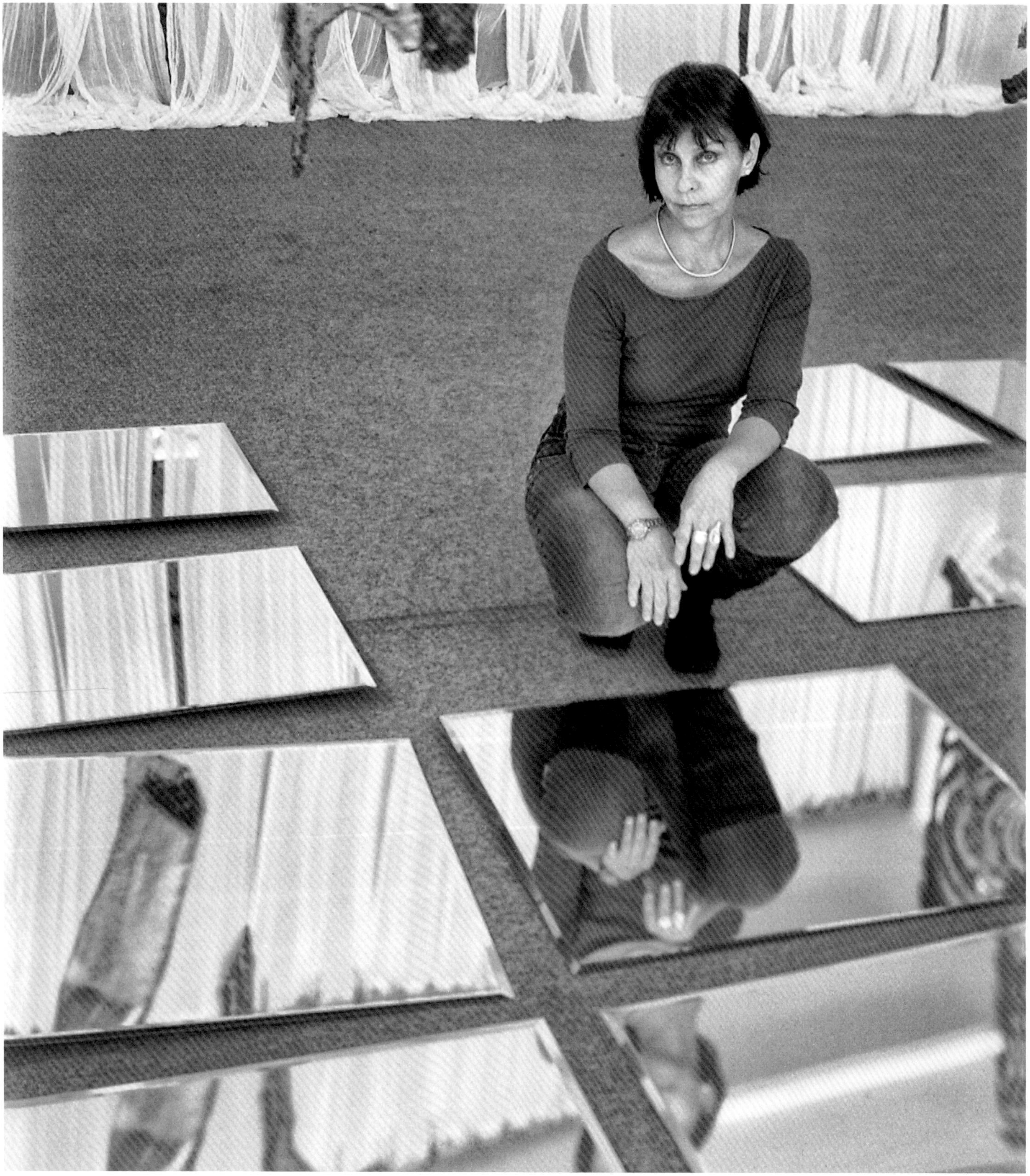

Becky Guttin

June, 2007

At the time I photographed Becky, she was in the midst of her sculptural installation with hanging pieces of metal reflected in mirrors on the floor. An intriguing conceptual use of materials, I found it stimulating to try to capture Becky as she was working out her installation exhibition. Some of the prints show her reflected with her work, others posing.

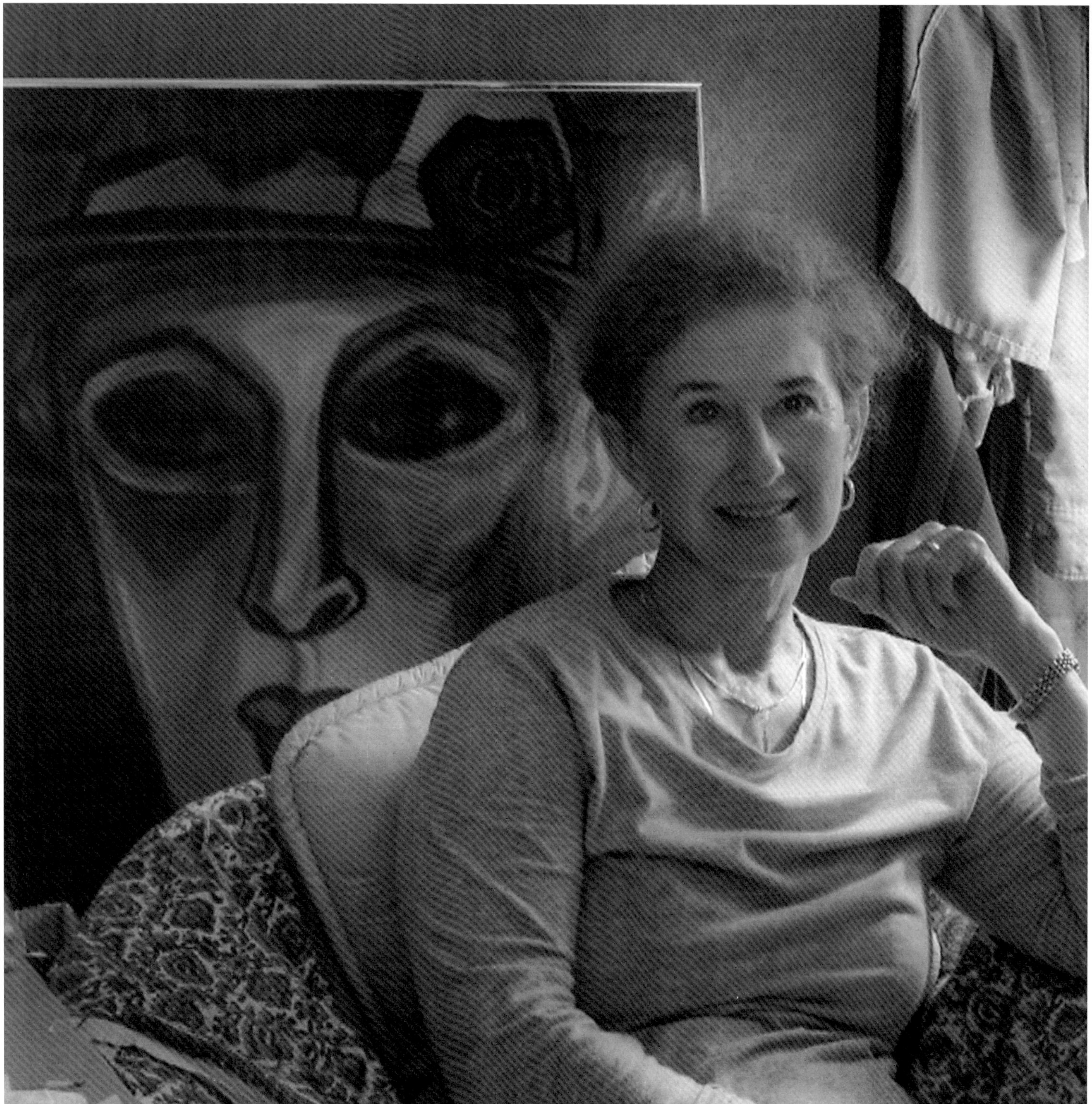

Nancy Kittredge

June, 2007

Soft-spoken Nancy invited me into her studio of large, impressive paintings. Powerful in color and design, they belie the gentleness of their creator. I began by watching Nancy move around in her studio, talking about what she was painting at the time, a series of magnificent, ethereal landscapes with angel-like characters and a mysterious light. While photographing Nancy, I noticed a skylight overhead, casting a light on Nancy's hair that made it look as if she could be one of the ethereal figures in her paintings with a glow of light about her head.

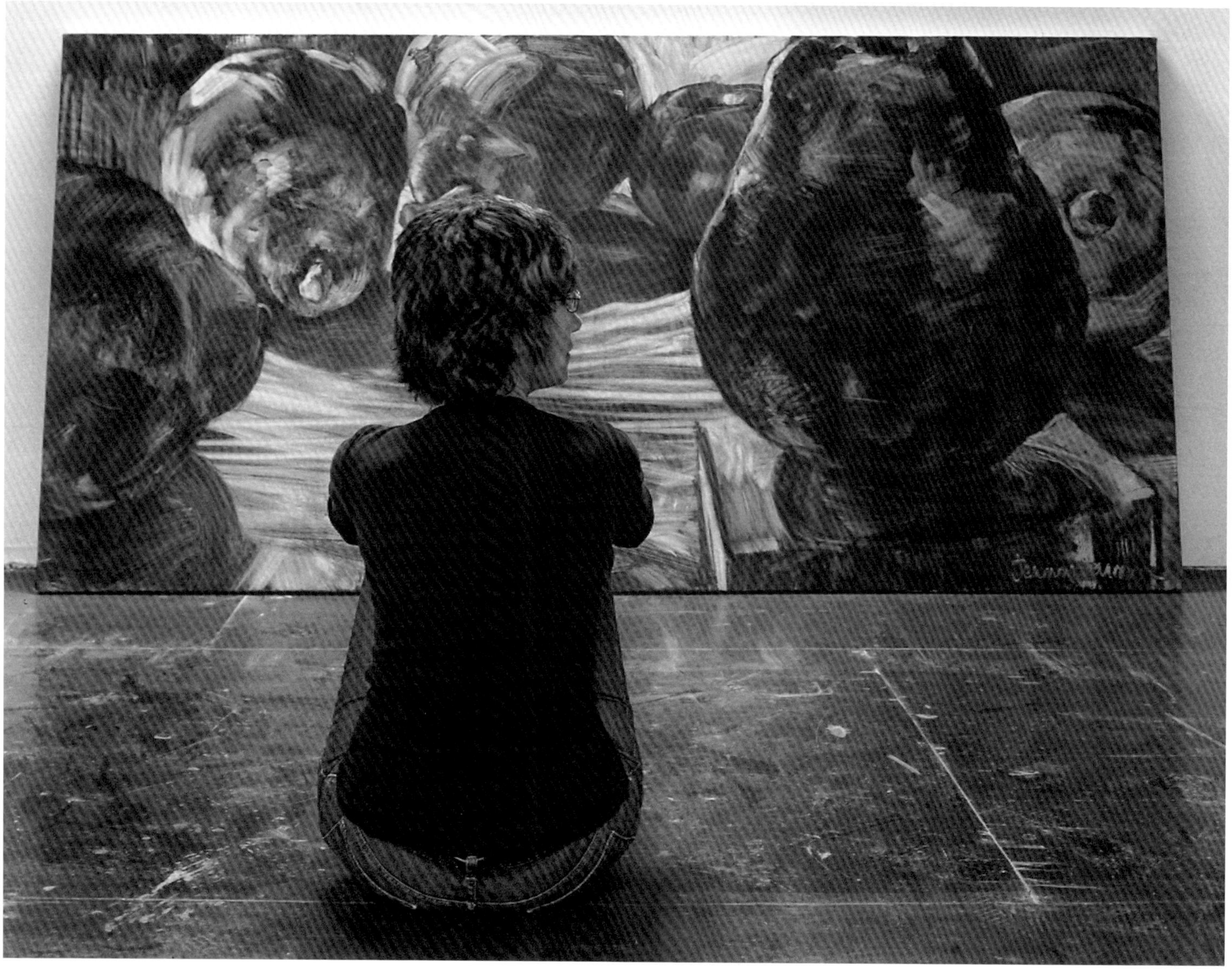

Jeanne Dunn

June, 2007

At the time I photographed Jeanne, she had recently moved into a new studio, much larger than the one she had in her home. The expanded space allowed me to see some of her larger works that displayed her playfulness in the use of everyday objects as symbols. What struck me about Jeanne and her large still-life painting was the similarity of the lush brushstrokes of the painting and the similar painterly quality of her hair coloring. (Call me weird, but that's what I saw.) Sitting her in front of her painting, I could picture her having a conversation with objects that could represent people, as though she were part of the painting.

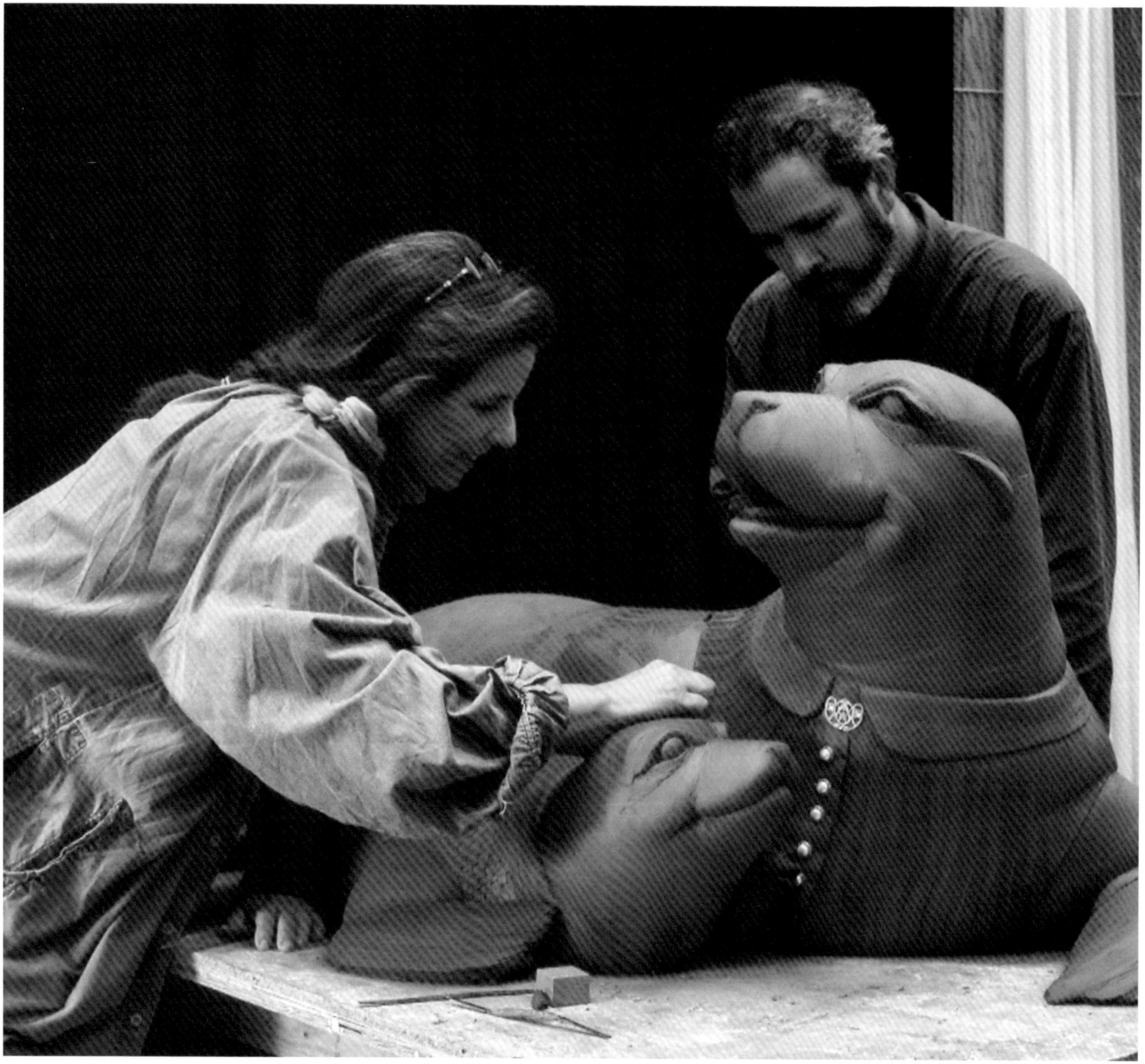

TJ Dixon and James Nelson

June, 2007

TJ Dixon and James Nelson are sculptors who specialize in large, figurative sculptures for public art. I met them both through a sculpture competition for Mission Trails Interpretative Center. They have developed a distinctive design that is featured in many public places. I'd never been to their studio, so it was quite a surprise seeing how they worked together to create their sculptures. Their working together is what I wanted to capture.

Suda House

November, 2009

I invited Suda to take part in the Movers & Shakers 2010 exhibition. As an inviter, I wanted to get a portrait of Suda for the show in January 2010 at the Art Expressions Gallery. We took each other's portraits for the show. Suda very cleverly installed my photo on a viewer and placed it inside of a large format camera body so that the viewer could see my image as they looked through the ground glass back. In turn, I created Suda's portrait image, scanned it to Pictoricio film and sandwiched the film between Plexiglas with a light source behind it. Suda had been working on her beautiful fabric photo pieces, creating undulating abstract imagery. She decided she wanted to become part of her piece, so I photographed her behind one of her translucent pieces with lighting off to the side. The image I produced for the exhibition was in color. I produced a second image of Suda as a platinum/palladium piece.

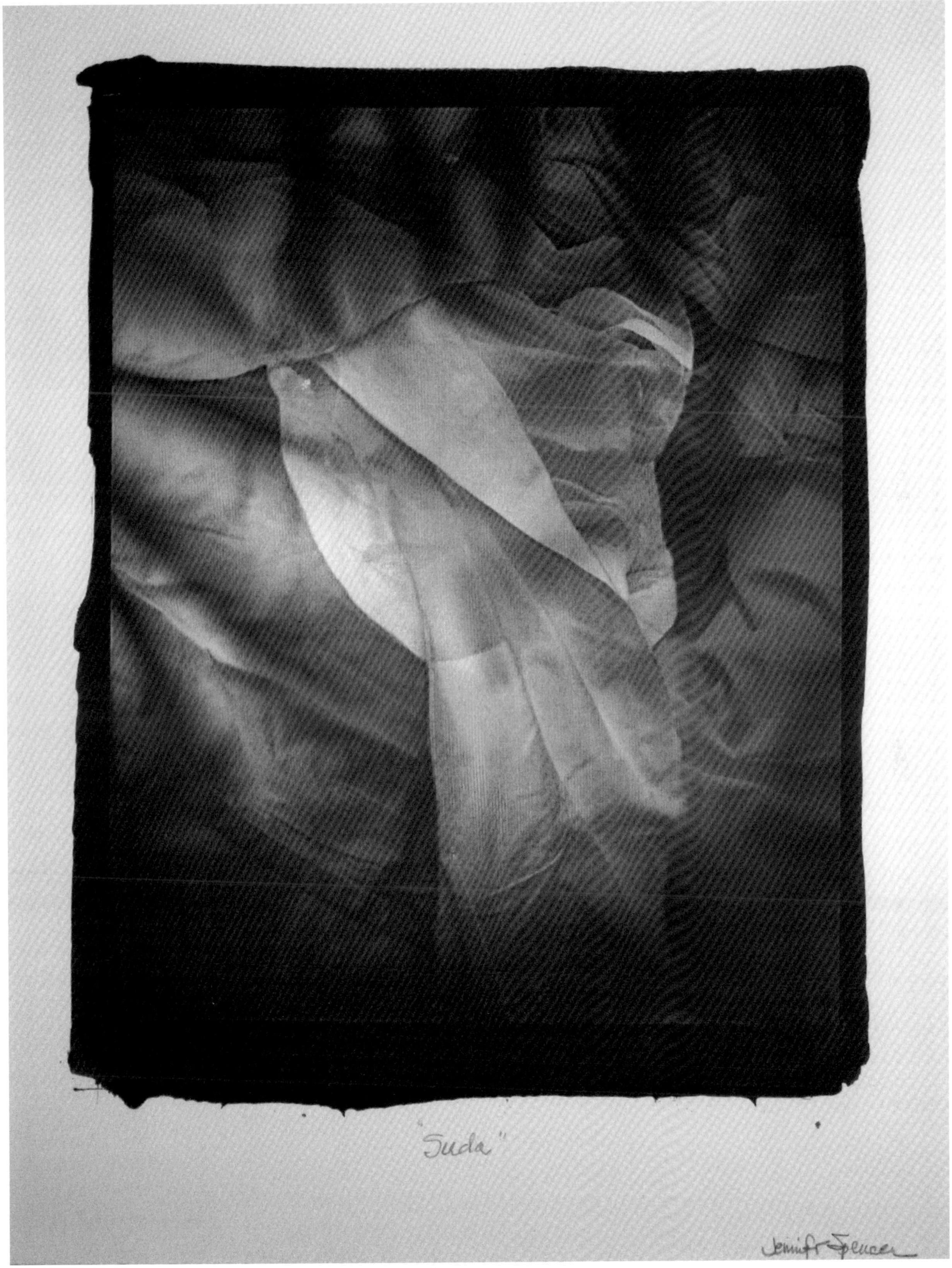
"Suda"

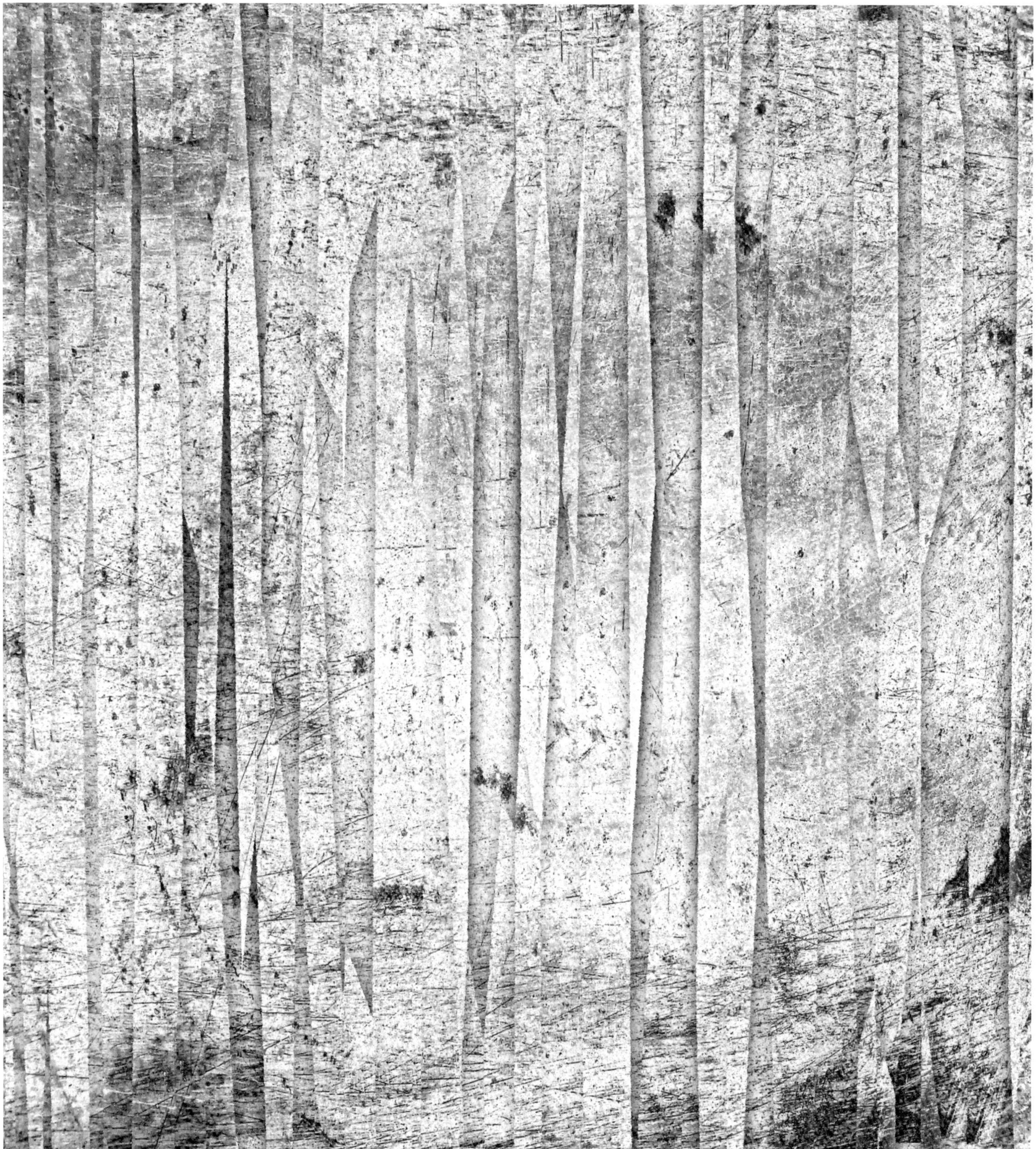

After a hiatus of almost five years for continuing education and concentration on landscape photography, I returned to my 4x5 film camera. I had been using my Canon digital for many of the landscape photographs I was taking while traveling. Though lighter and easier to set up, the digital camera did not produce the kind of depth I was looking for in my photographs. I was becoming less enamored with my digital camera and more dissatisfied with just photographing landscapes. There had to be more to hold my curiosity and my need for creative fulfillment. I rediscovered film. The images in black and white were more intriguing, especially for portraits.

Returning to portraiture, I began trying to make connections with artists and wasn't having much success until I discovered Facebook. Fortunately, I got lucky and connected with most of the artists I knew when I was an ED of a non-profit arts organization, COVA (Combined Organizations for the Visual Arts). Many artists have also discovered Facebook as a method of getting their work out and keeping in touch with other artists. The online platform for artist exposure was growing. As such, gallery representation is often difficult to come by.

Since I was a bit rusty, I contacted friends Jess and Mary Lynn Dominguez to be my first portrait subjects. They were both wonderfully supportive and cooperative in letting me capture their images on film. Because my work did not please me that day, I arranged to re-shoot them later in their studios. Early on in my portraiture adventure, I discovered that my digital camera proved useful in previewing the setting for each portrait shoot. It also became a wonderful diversionary tool to distract the portrait sitter. I was beginning to use more of the techniques famed photographer Arnold Newman utilized to get his sitter to relax and reveal the "essence" of who they are.

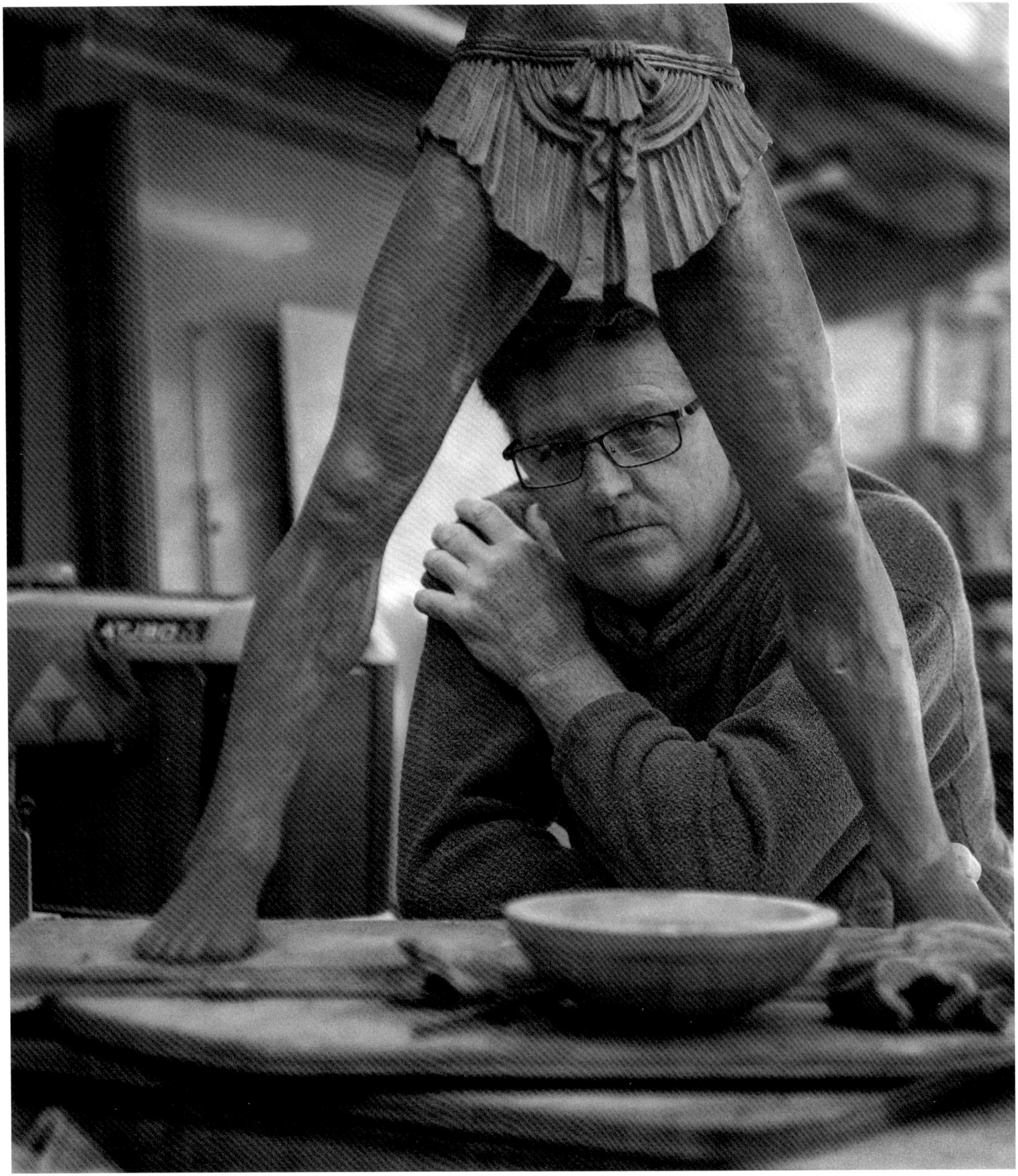

Chris Lee

March, 2014

Fresh off my artist portrait hiatus, photographing Chris Lee in his studio was a challenge. Chris is one of those artists who likes to work with others and is always most generous. He made some useful suggestions. There were so many areas that would that would work for his portrait, it was difficult to decide. From outside in his work area, filled with tools and materials, to inside his home with some of his finished pieces, it was a challenge trying to find where he felt most comfortable being photographed. We settled on his outside workspace, where he was in the process of finishing the model for a large piece going into a private residence—his Colossus of Rhoades.

Ron Tatro

March, 2014

Ron is a sculptor who incorporates color into his sculptures in a unique way that is also reflected in his design work and drawings. In the traditional Italian way, Ron and his wife Janet invited me to a lovely lunch after Ron's portrait work. We talked about how their home burned during the Crest fire that left them homeless, leaving only the studio standing. They have since built a beautiful new home with a fabulous view of East County. At this time, I learned about one of Ron's earlier works that found its way back to him. Like many artists who go through cycles, Ron has done the same, and is recapturing some of his earlier design work. Reflecting Ron's encounter with an earlier work is how I chose to capture him at that moment. Using three different negatives for the final image in a composite, I, framed the image using the Ilford 400 negative frame.

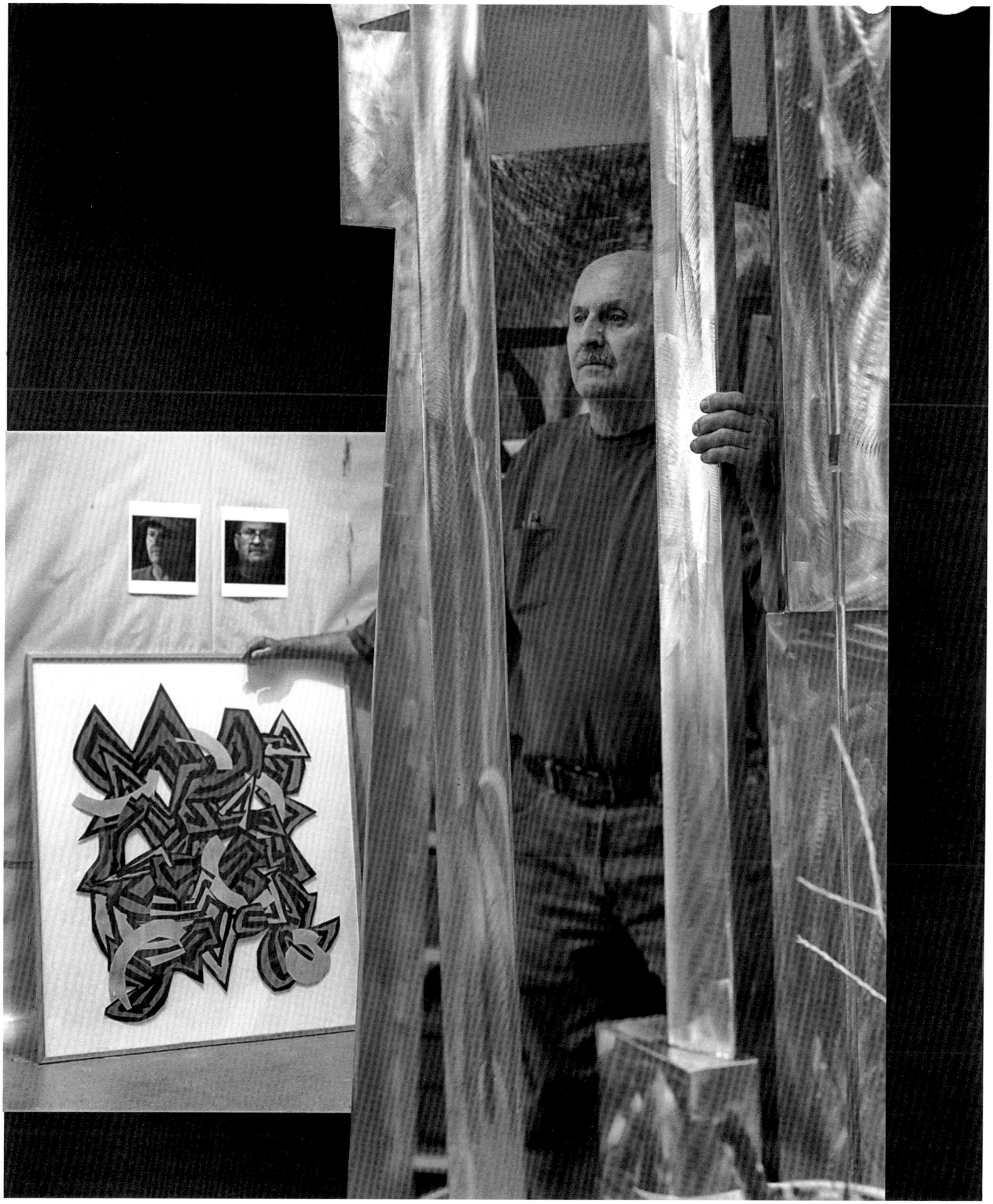

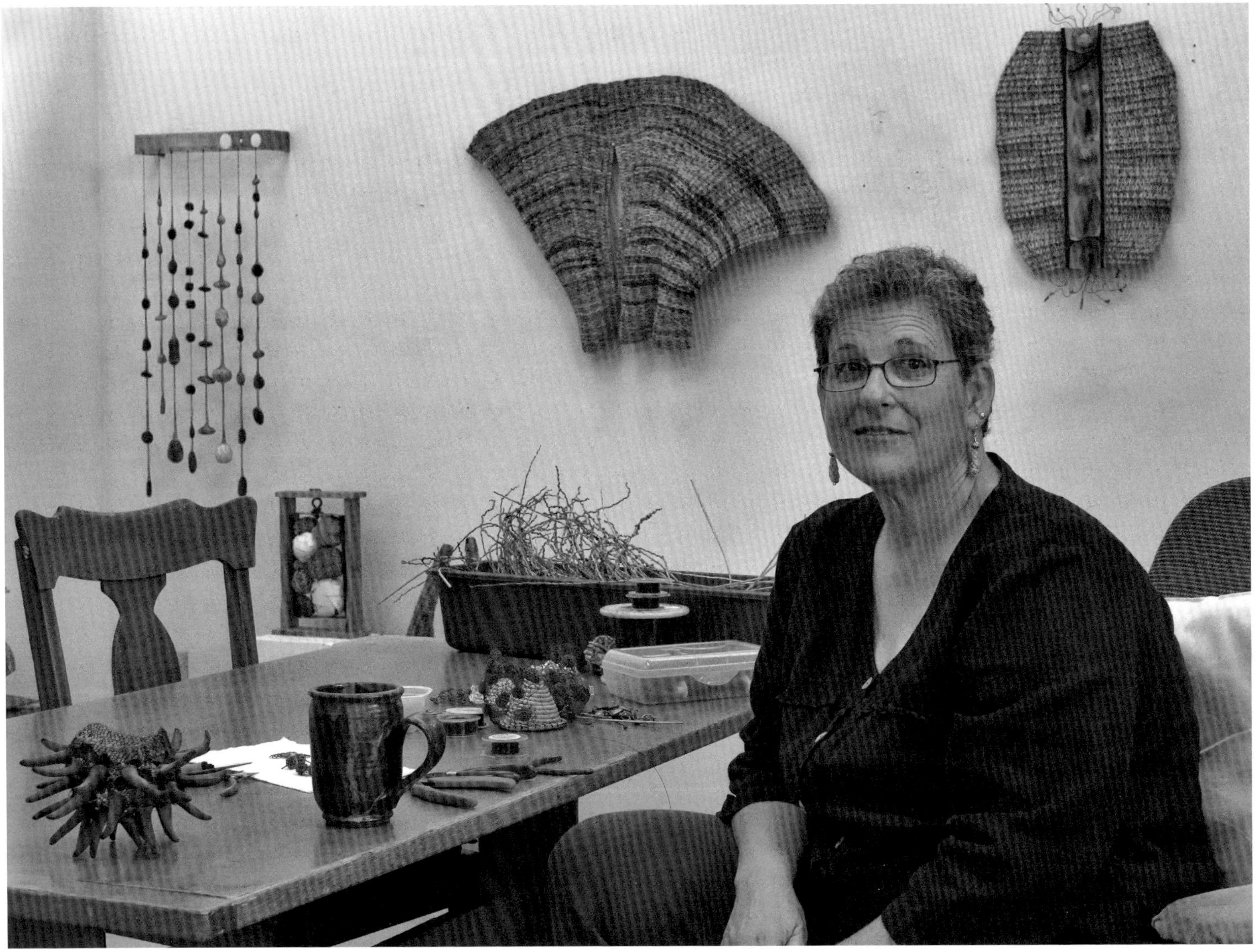

Polly Jacobs Giacchina

April, 2014

Sometime in the early '80s, Polly and I had a show together at the Spectrum Gallery. The underwater theme we chose featured her weavings, representing deep sea sponges and other creatures, while I showed my tectonic plate painting. We even created some pieces together. I still have one of them in my studio. Polly's style has remained the organic interpretation of life around her in elegant, beautifully woven patterns.

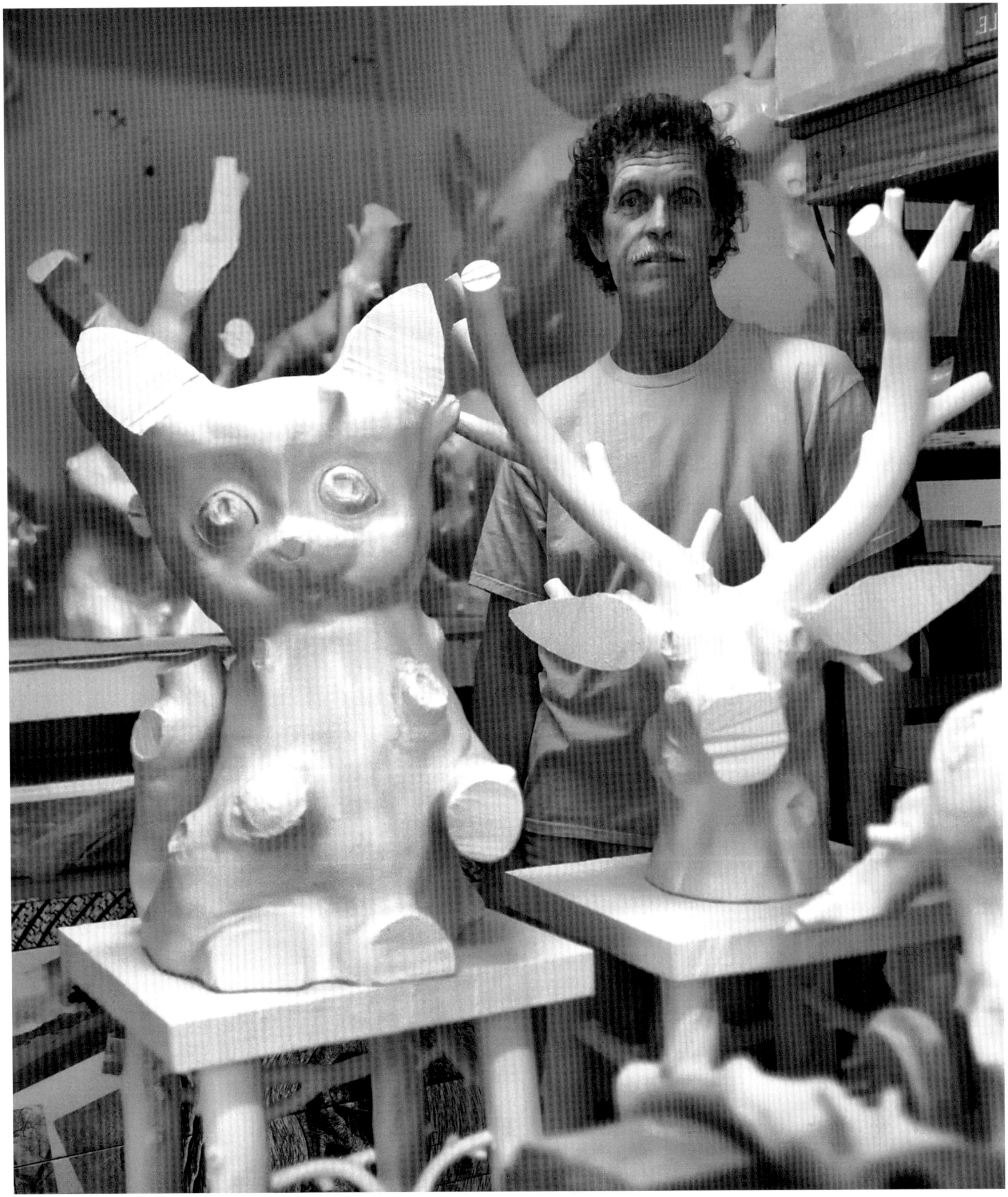

Jeff Irwin

April, 2014

Upon walking into Jeff's studio, the first thing I saw was a white-on-white study, with many of his ceramic sculpture animal heads hanging on walls like trophies or on shelves against white walls. In another room, there were other painted ceramic sculptures. Though a sad commentary on the killing of animals and displaying them as trophies, there seemed to be a bit of dark humor evident in being surrounded by his work that fit Jeff's personality, so I placed him as one of "the trophies," stacked in a corner.

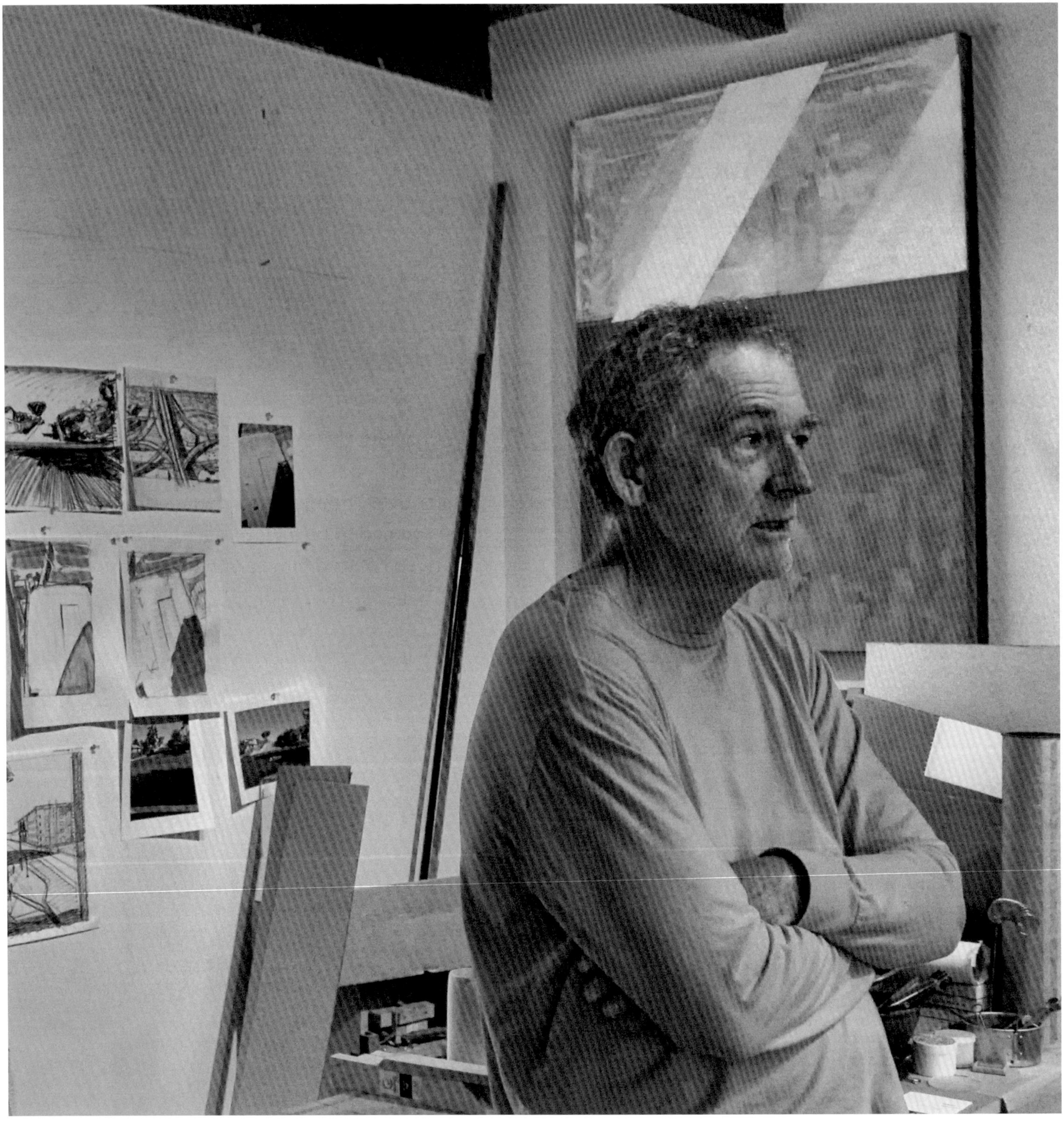

Bill Mosley

May, 2014

Laconic, laid-back Bill was a study in relaxed curiosity. I always admired his landscapes of highways under construction, like Highway 125 in East County, and his high-rise downtown San Diego paintings. Teaching full-time at Grossmont College doesn't allow many art instructors time for their own work, so I was pleasantly surprised to see new work in progress. The studio is part of his home. After catching up a bit, I began to recognize a look and posture he would have in class. He explained that he now dresses less casually since he gets more respect and attention from students. With his study drawings in the background, it looked like a good pose for him. His portrait is of him as if he were before a class of students.

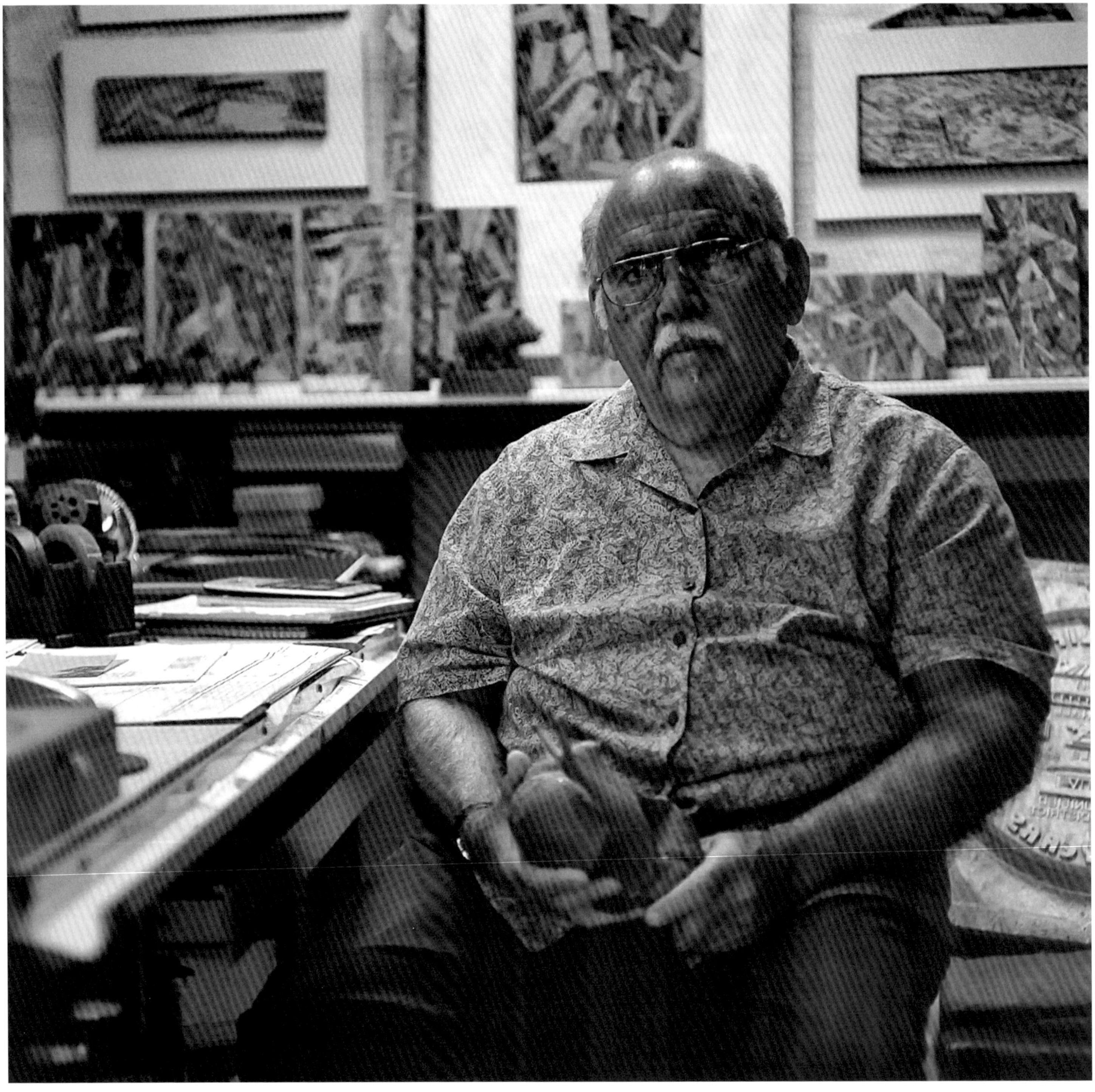

Jess & Mary Lynn Dominguez

June, 2014

Good artist friends, Jess and Mary Lynn, were very welcoming when I asked to do their portraits. And I even returned to capture them in a different light. Though they have very different styles and ways of working, when they work together on a project, it sings of harmony. Currently working on an installation for downtown La Mesa, they had drawings and mockup pieces ready to show. Now, just being patient seems to be the biggest challenge for them, as it is for most public artists.

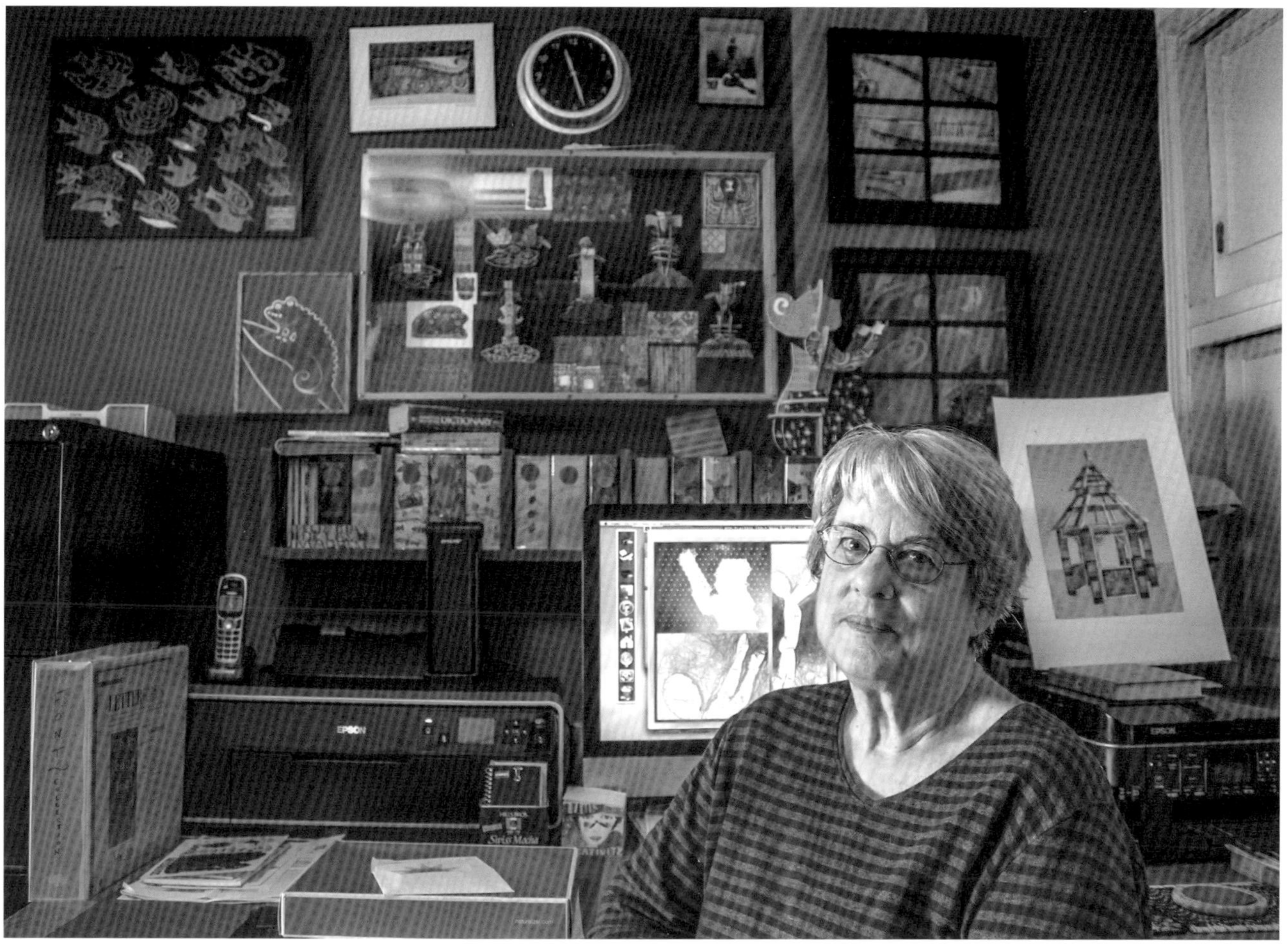

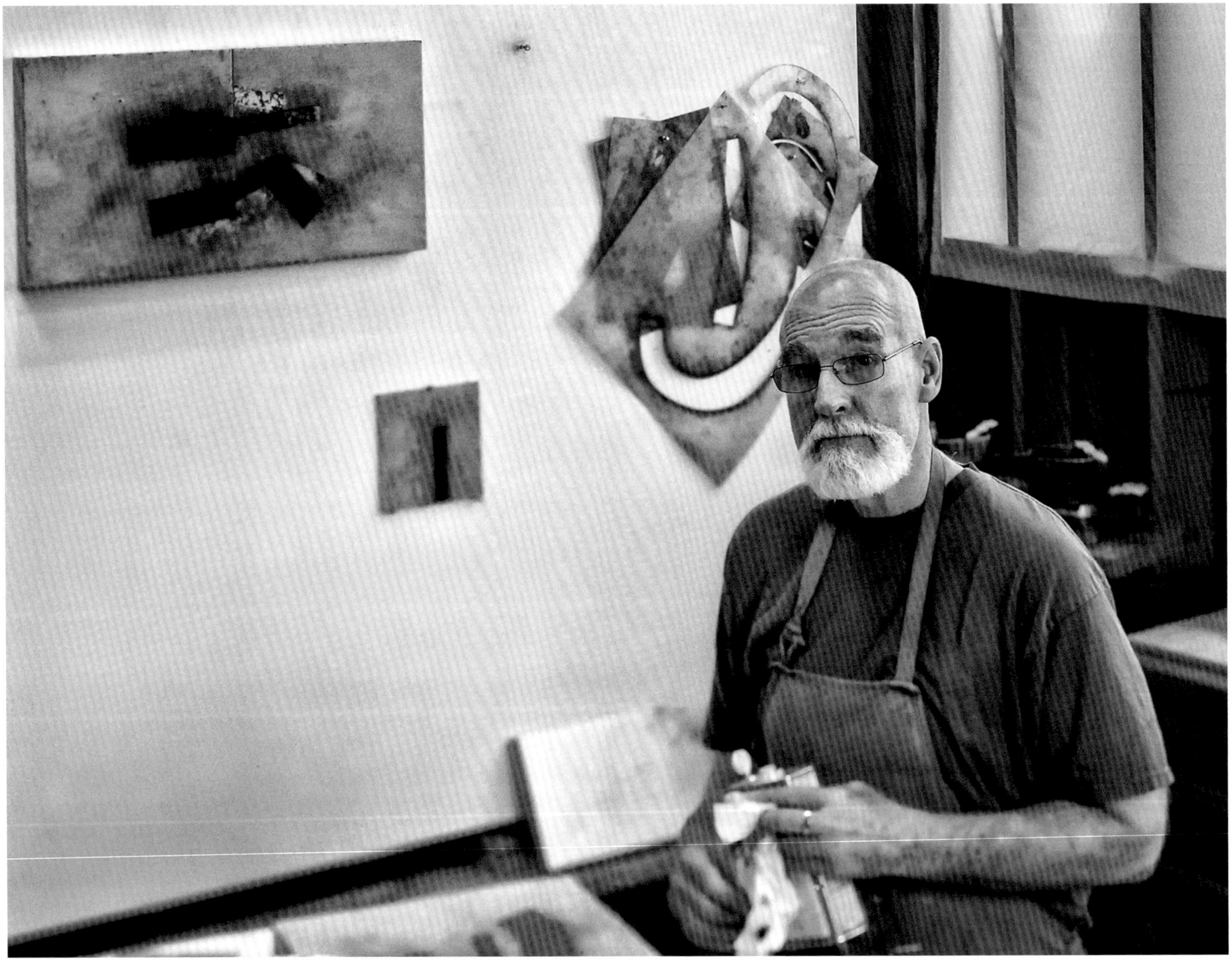

Robert Treat

June, 2014

I'd never been to Bob Treat's studio, but always was curious about his encaustic process and elegant work. The process looked like a way to combine painting with photography, something I've struggled to do. During our photo session, I discovered that Bob was looking at moving closer to photography from the encaustic paintings he'd been doing for several years. What an interesting discourse followed, both of us trying to find ways to meld the two processes. He's now moving more into photography, with drama and mystery in each image.

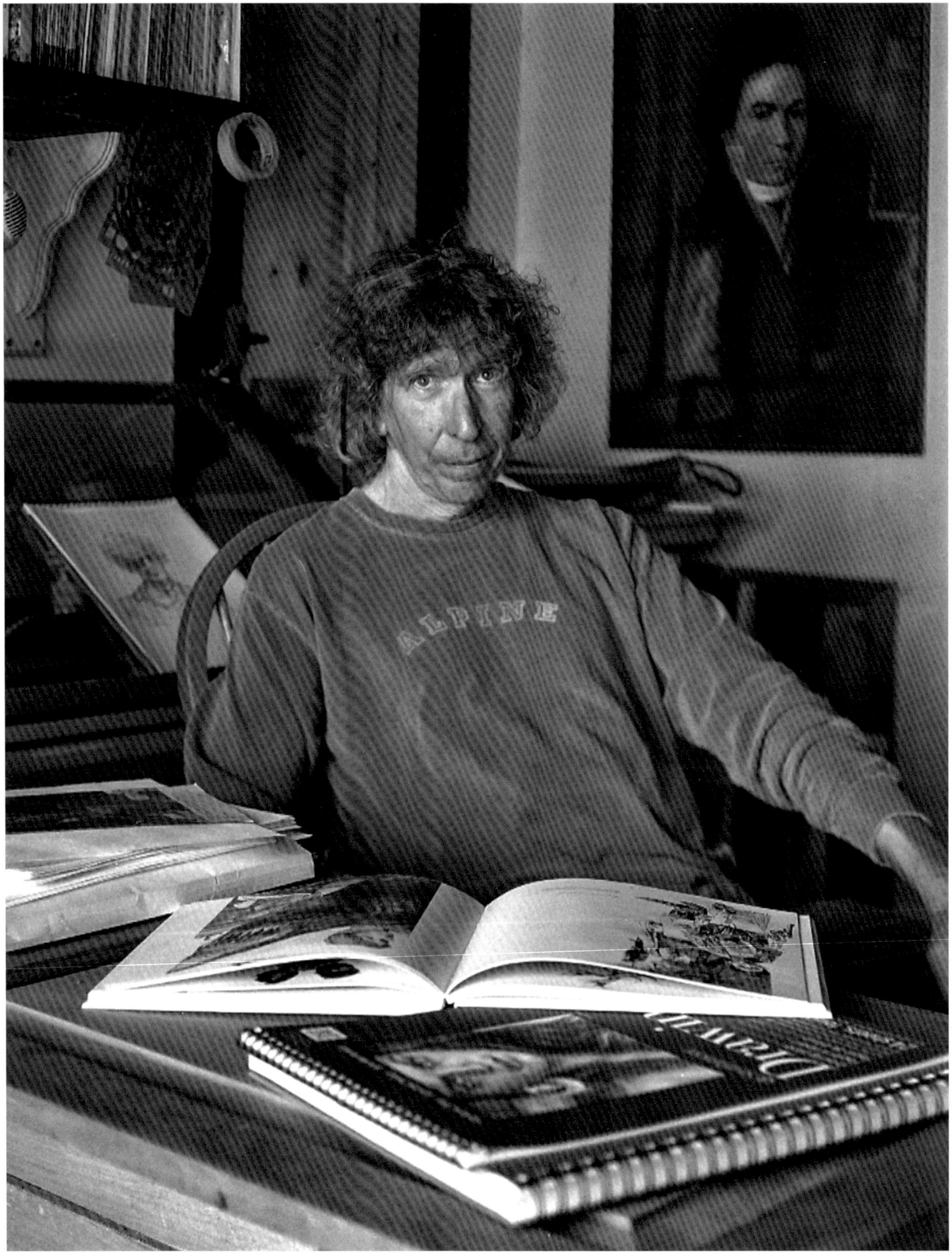
ALPINE

Jay Abel

July, 2014

Jay looks like a character in one of his drawings . . . that can sometimes have a wry sense of humor with dark trappings. His studio is his whole house. Windows covered (it's hot out today). Everywhere one looks one sees a drawing pad and pens. Books are everywhere as well. I feel as if I'm in a kind of museum diorama. It isn't until we step outside into the heat that Jay shows me his new "baby," a vintage car, recently purchased. Digitally I photographed him with his "new baby" and gave him the photo to celebrate his new purchase.

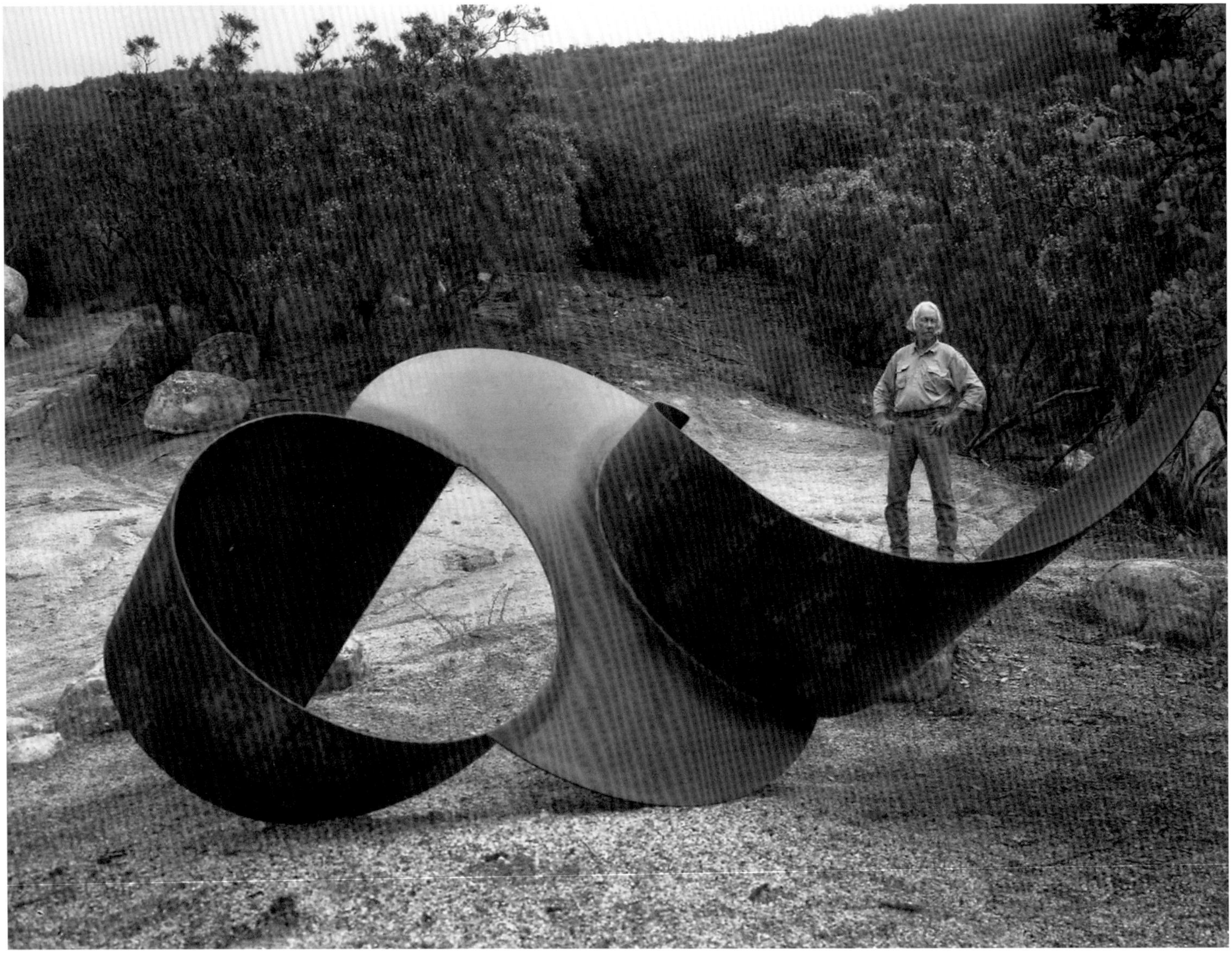

Kenneth Capps

August, 2014

On an overcast muggy morning, I was to meet up with Kenneth Capps at his property, a foundation for his sculpture. Perfect lighting for an outdoor portrait shoot, one of the very few I've done for artists. Halfway through the session, rain began to pour down hard, causing us to immediately pack up and run to his truck for shelter. As I sat chatting with Kenneth and his lovely wife back at their cabin, the rain began to let up. Looking over at my damp equipment and cameras, I suddenly realized I'd left the bag with my film cartridges under a little tree where we were shooting. OMG! Rain may have ruined all my work! Kenneth jumped up, dashed out the door to his truck, sped over to where we had been and retrieved the plastic bag containing my films. Rushing back, he deposited the wet bag on a towel and I proceeded to haul out each film cartridge for inspection. Luckily, the bag was closed and only a little wetness was present. I had only one more cartridge left to expose. Kenneth suggested, to finish, we go behind their little cabin for a shot near a huge boulder. While shooting earlier, I noticed that Kenneth kept moving away from the sculpture, placing himself in the background. He didn't want a close-up of himself, only a shot of his work. Well, that shot behind the cabin did the trick. Got the close-up. No film was damaged in the production of this portrait shoot. Whew! The portrait I selected of Kenneth is the one where his work is front and center, with him appearing to stand in the swoop of the piece. Although the close-up of Kenneth was saved, I felt that the portrait of him, much smaller than his work, better expressed in essence who Kenneth is—an artist who prefers his art seen and not him.

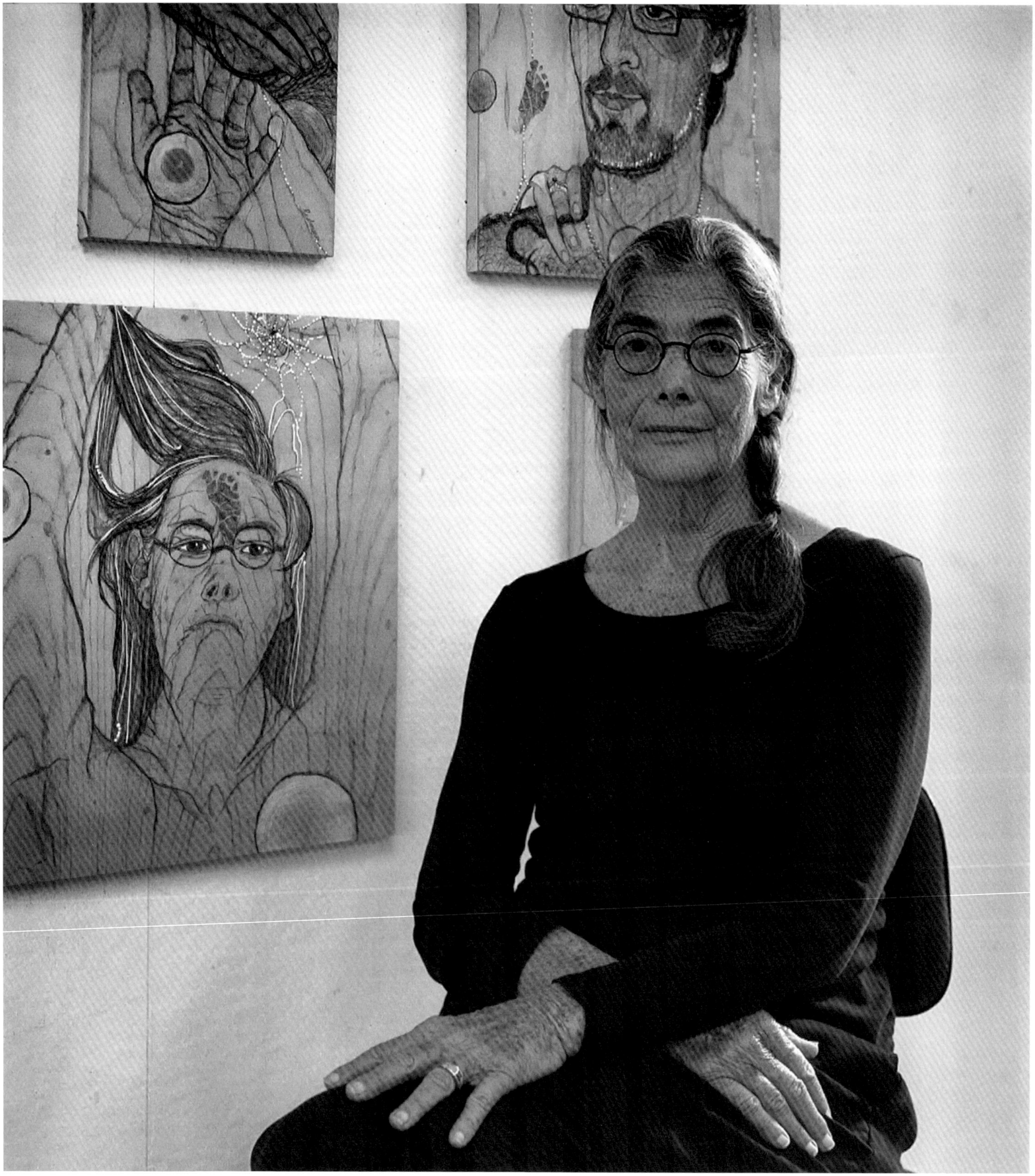

Helen Redman

November, 2014

When I appeared for her portrait shoot, Helen was in a state of hectic preparation for two upcoming shows at the Women's Museum and Mesa College. I was glad she could give me some time and had a great catch-up conversation about art and family. Helen is a whirlwind with definite plans about how things should be done, intense and yet very vulnerable. This is reflected in her work. Fortunately, I was able to capture her in a more meditative pose, while a little pensive.

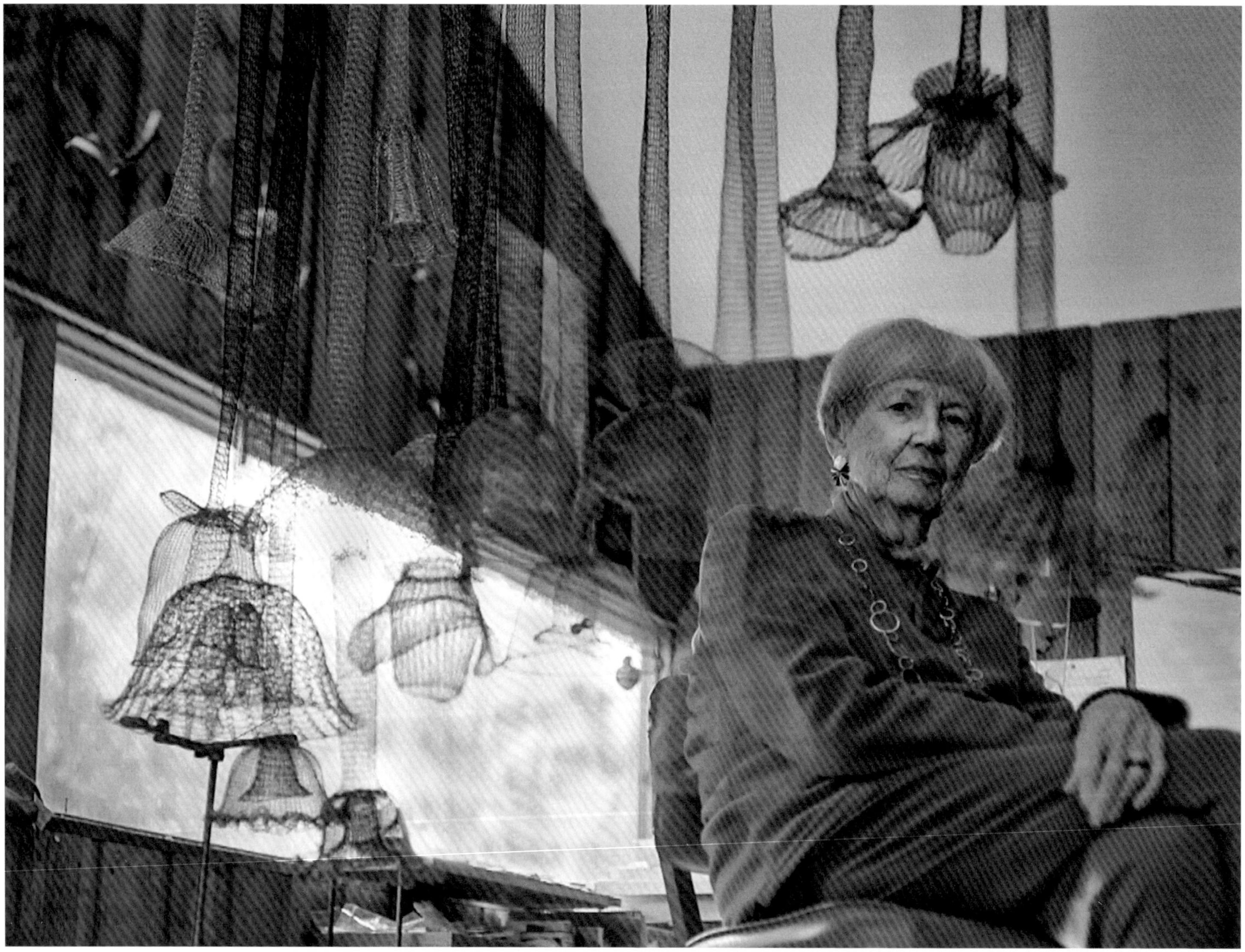

Arline Fisch

November, 2014

Arline, colorfully dressed, welcomed me into her multilevel home. Her studio is on a lower level. Her work is as colorful as she is, so it was a challenge to capture her with her work in black and white. Hanging on different levels of her studio were some of her recent work from an exhibition. I decided to design a frame of her work around her, reflecting how her work surrounds her in her workspace, with all of her metal-fiber working tools.

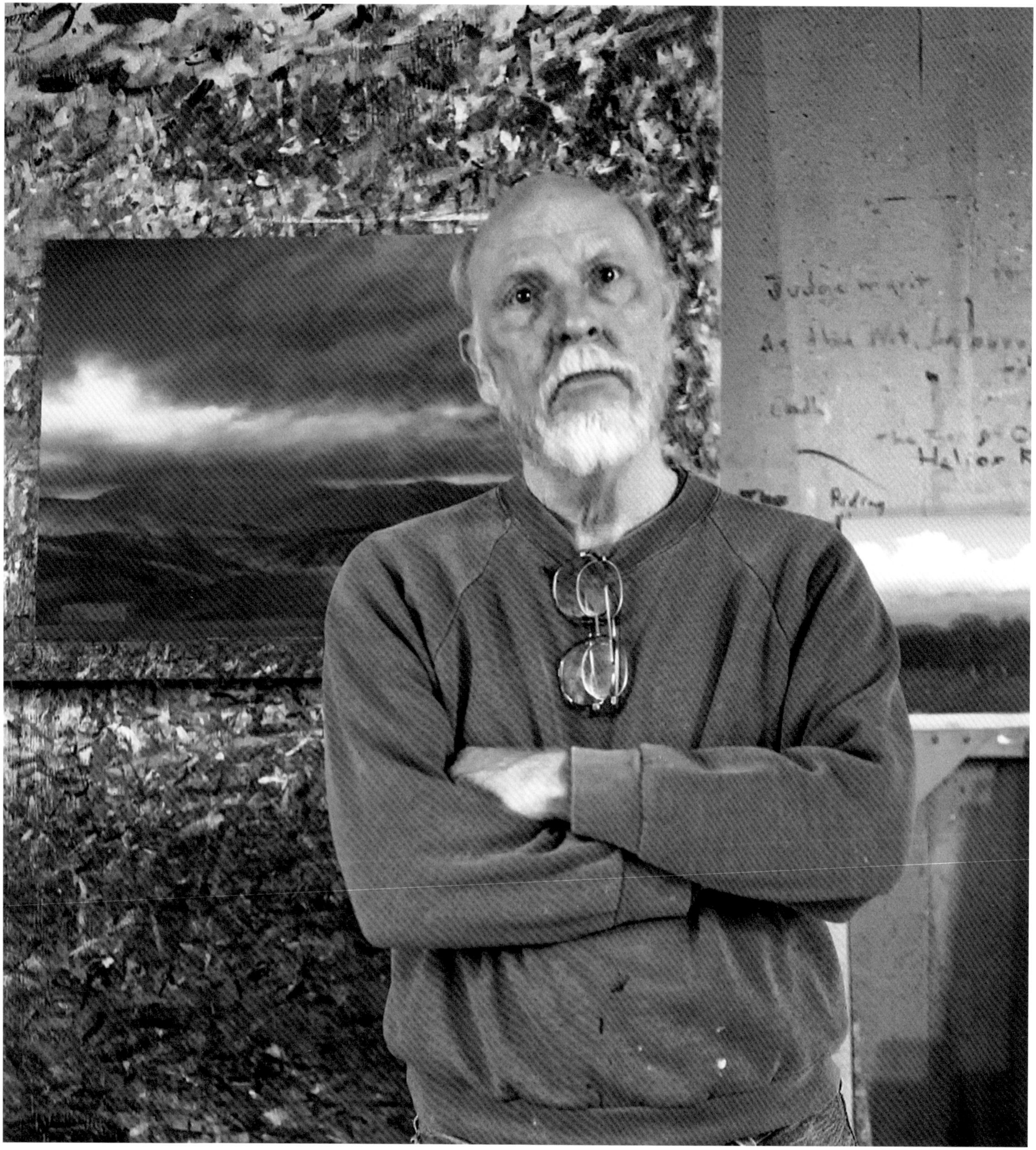

William Glen Crooks

January, 2015

Prolific landscape painter William Glen Crooks has a vision of an environment that is slowly slipping away. A bit of nostalgia in his wonderfully rendered landscapes makes you wish for other days, for time to just wander the landscape and marvel. He has, in some respects, become part of his landscapes. I wanted to capture that quality, as though he has melted into his landscapes.

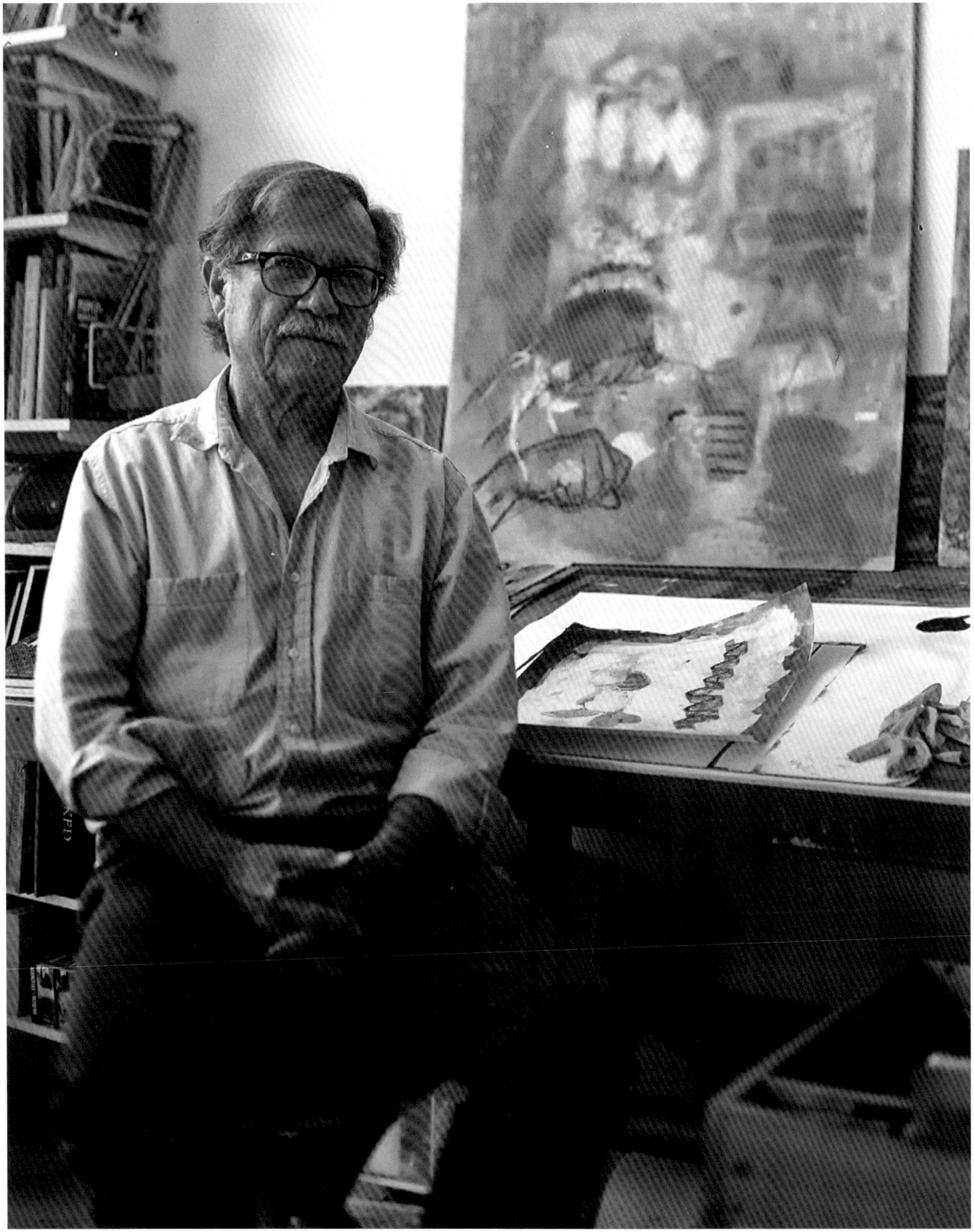

James Aitchison

January, 2015

Painter James Aitchinson's work often has references to the written word, either poetry or prose. The paintings seem to be telling a story that draws you in, just as James does as he quotes poems in relation to what's on his mind. A very thoughtful artist, expressing himself on paper or canvas is sometimes a game of responding to what goes on the surface as he contemplates what it means, trying to be honest with himself.

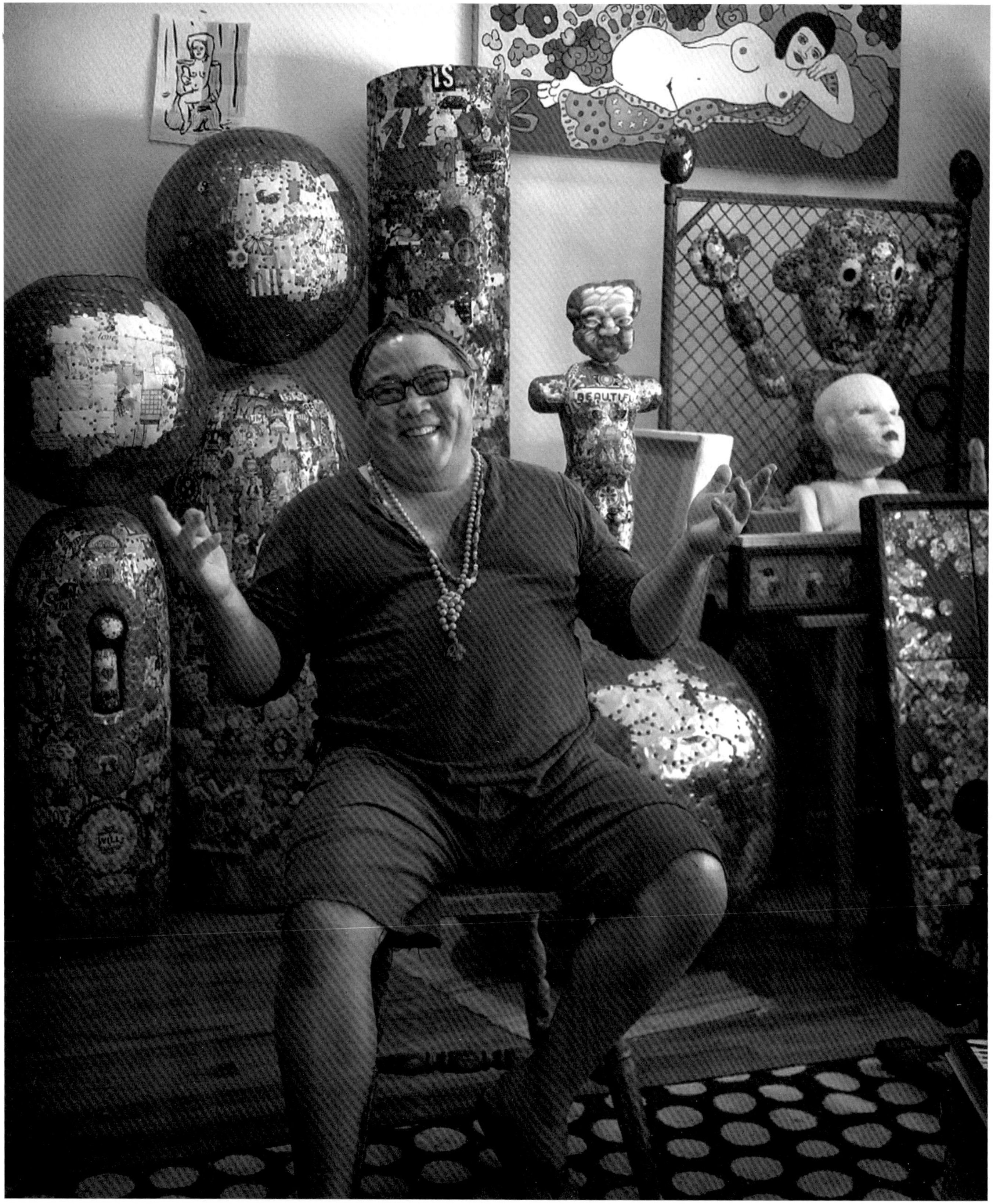
IS
BEAUTIF

James Watts

February, 2015

James is an artist's artist, living in downtown San Diego in a storefront space that serves as studio, gallery, and living quarters. How rare is that today! The lifestyle definitely suits James's outgoing, freethinking style of unique sculpture and paintings. Always intrigued by James's infectious fun-loving and outgoing nature, I was not surprised to find him quite literally at home in his space. Kibitzing with passersby and his neighbors, he is well respected in his neighborhood. James's sculptures or figures look like his "family," as they are placed around his home and gallery. Capturing this good-natured yet serious artist was a challenge, determining which side of him to portray.

Susan J. Osborn

February, 2015

Susan, is a multi-media artist and teacher. Initially, I had an opportunity to know her better when I did sub work for her in her art classes at the Bishop School in La Jolla. I'd never been to her studio/home before. Surveying the small studio below the living quarters, I happened to glance outside and see a small, strange-looking structure. Susan's work can be somewhat mysterious and whimsical, and the little structure said it all. She's an artist who makes you wonder what's going through her head as she works.

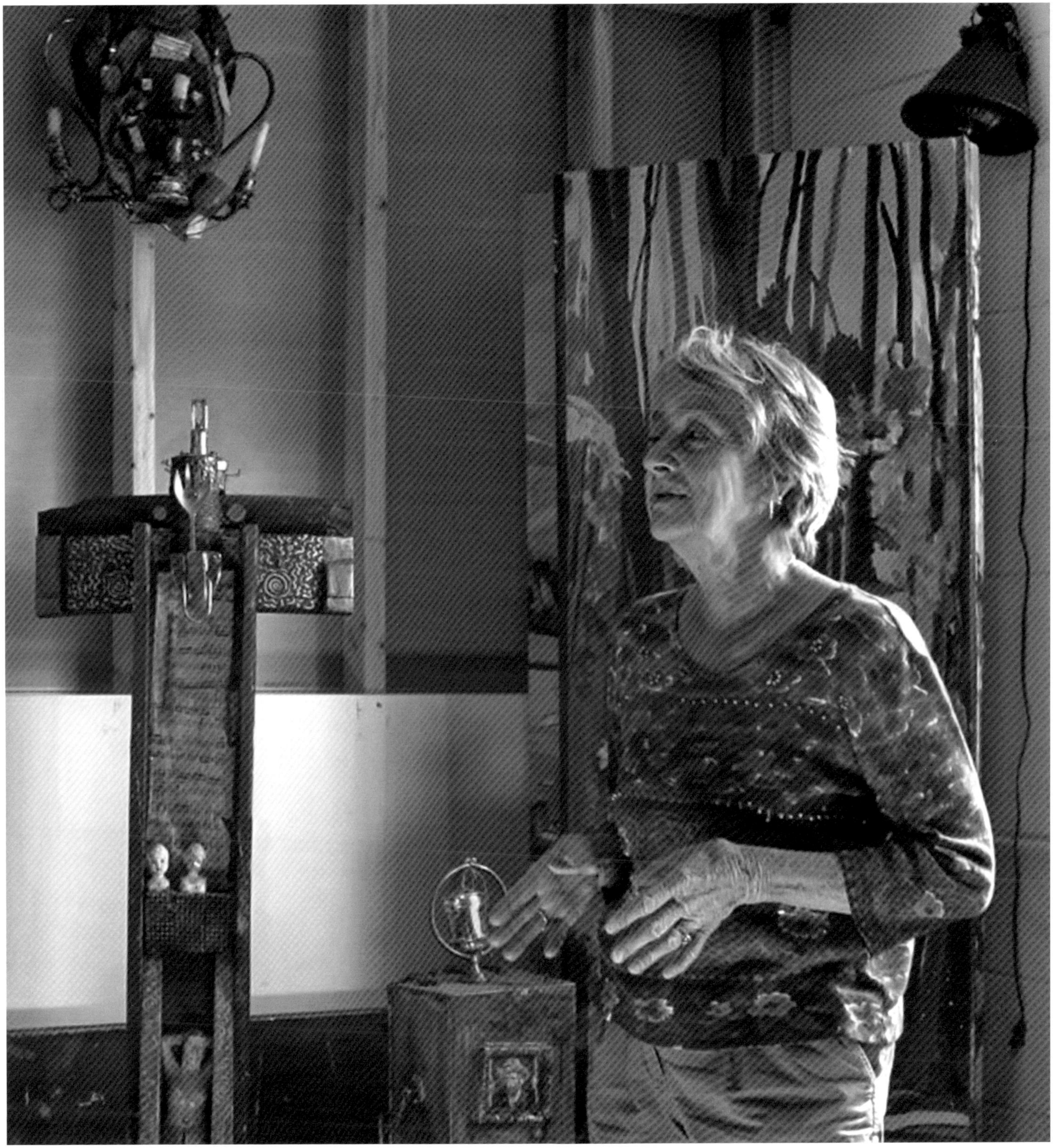

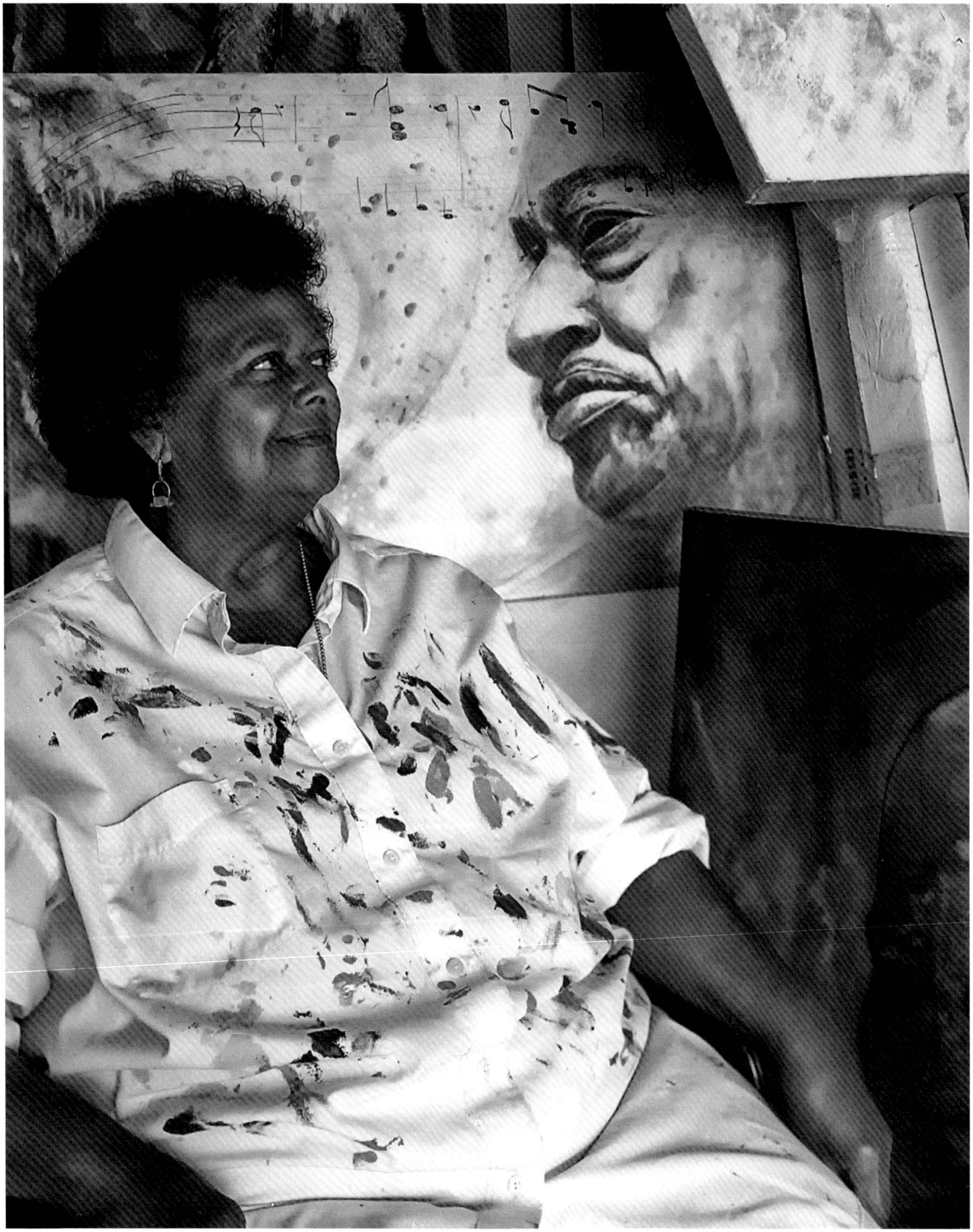

Jean Cornell Wheat

February, 2015

Many years ago, as I was just beginning my portrait project, I photographed Jean in her home on the San Pasqual Academy grounds where she was an art instructor for foster youth. My first portraits of her were shot with my 35mm film camera. I decided to do a follow-up portrait of her using my 4x5 film field camera, like all the others in the series. Amazing that Jean has not changed much in over nine years. A caring artist with a talent for working with young people, she is still at the San Pasqual Academy, but now as a "grandparent" to the foster kids. She greets you with a quick smile and a wonderful laugh.

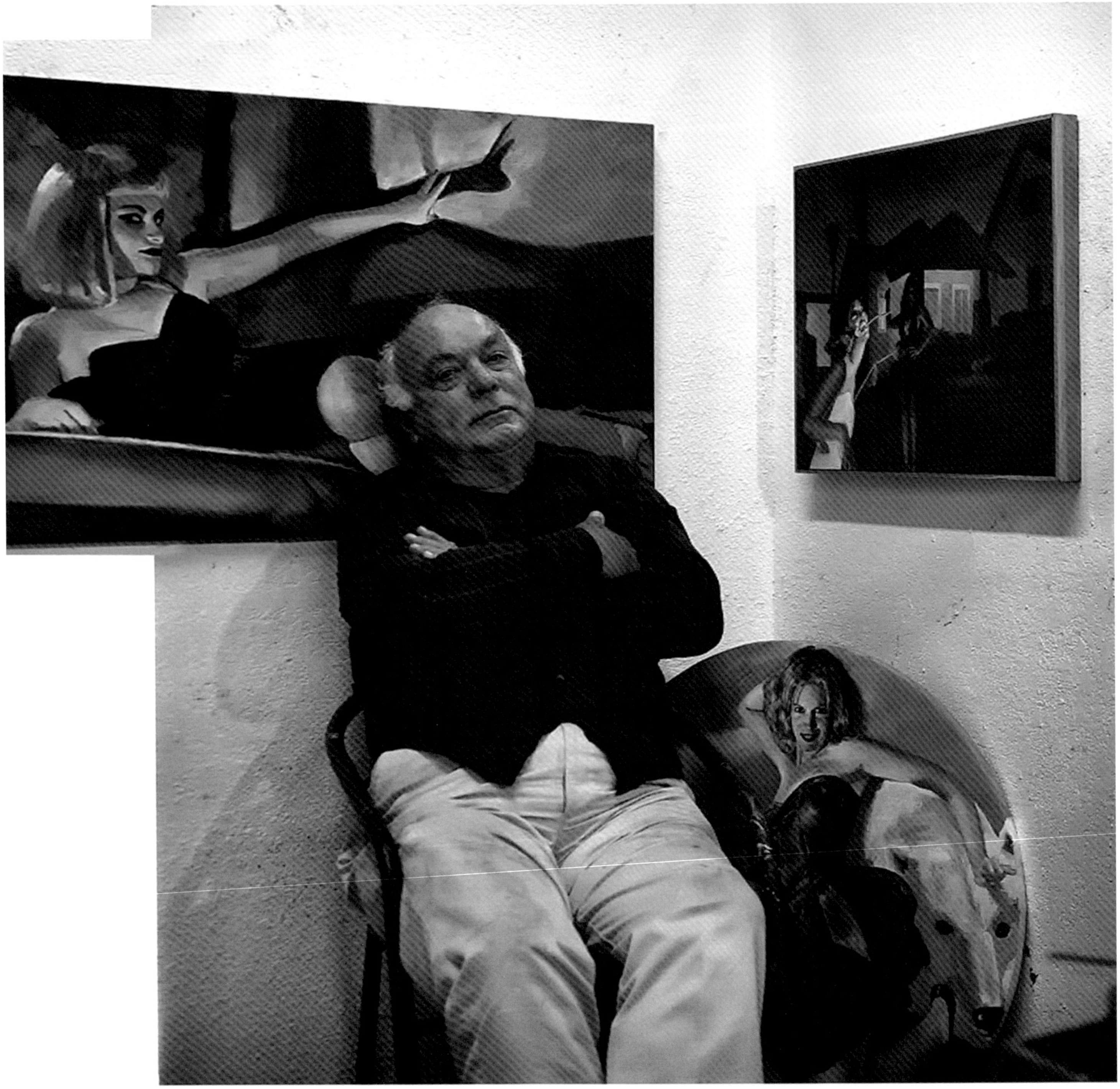

Dan Camp

March, 2015

Dan, a prolific painter and instructor, has over the years developed a unique style that has always intrigued me. It had been some time since I had last seen Dan. I'd never gone to his studio, the new one he has in downtown San Diego. Though Dan's studio is compact in size, with paintings stacked to one side, it offered a challenge to capture Dan in close quarters compared to the larger studio he had before. Sometimes close quarters force one to concentrate more closely on detail and emphasize design, like a stage setting . . . as in his paintings.

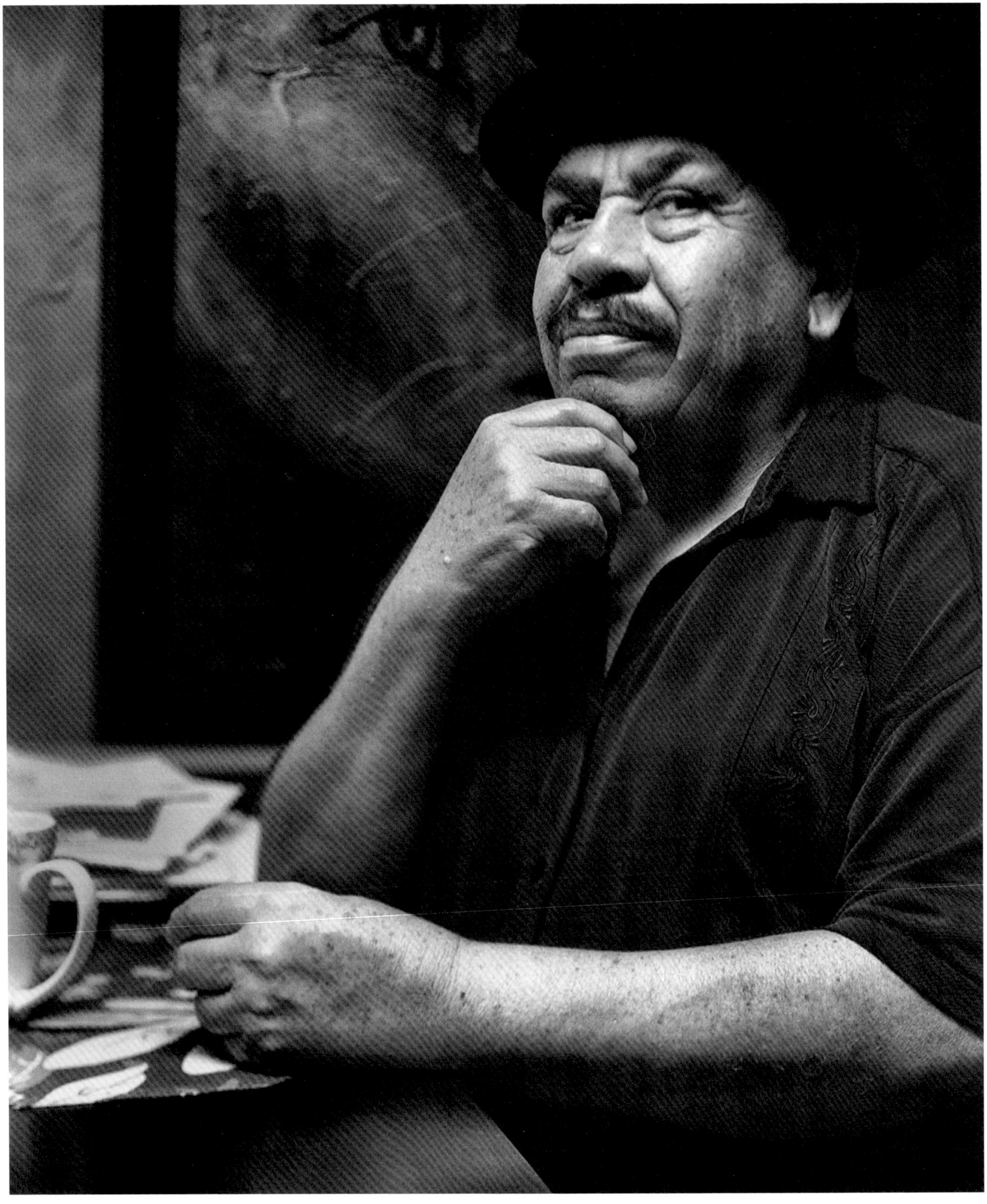

Victor Ochoa

April, 2015

Victor, the well-known and celebrated muralist of Chicano Park fame, has been photographed many times. Many paintings have also been done of him, and photographs of him working on murals, but no formal portraits that I know of. It was going to be a challenge for me to find some new way to see him. Because his work is mostly on site, when he does do work on paintings in his home, many of them are very large in a small space.

Even though I've known Victor for some time in the art community, there were many things I didn't know that were revealed during our photo session. Victor is quite the storyteller as well as artist. As the portrait session progressed, I was regaled with many stories about his work with other Chicano artists in the community over the years and his activism in establishing Chicano Park.

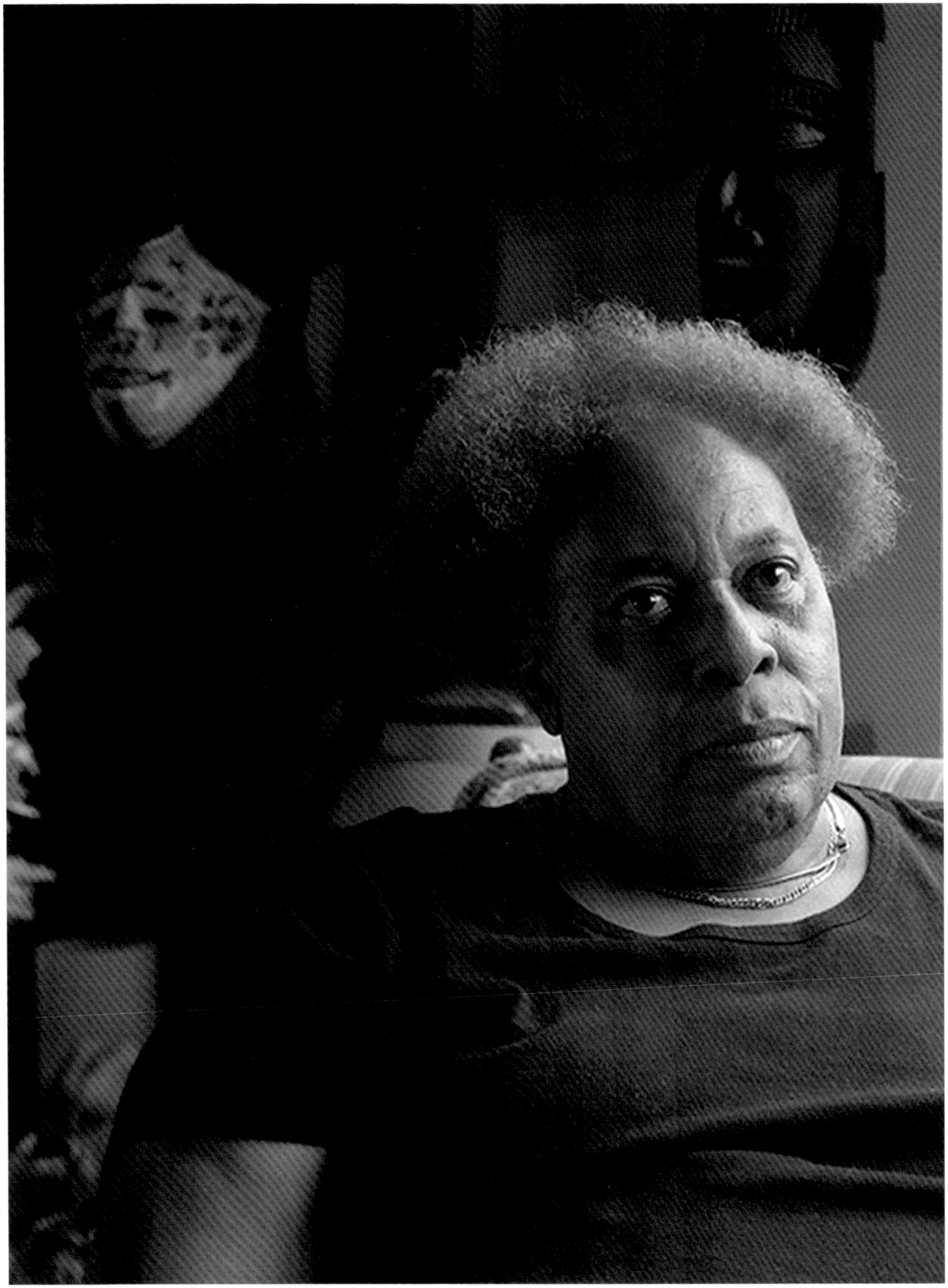

Ric Todd

April, 2015

Ric is not only an administrator of art programs, but also an artist. His whole house appeared to be his studio, with art pieces everywhere you looked, amongst his own art collection. Ric has a wonderful sense of humor . . . and lots of stories. It was good to catch up and learn of his recent position on the San Diego Art Institute Board and the challenges the organization was dealing with.

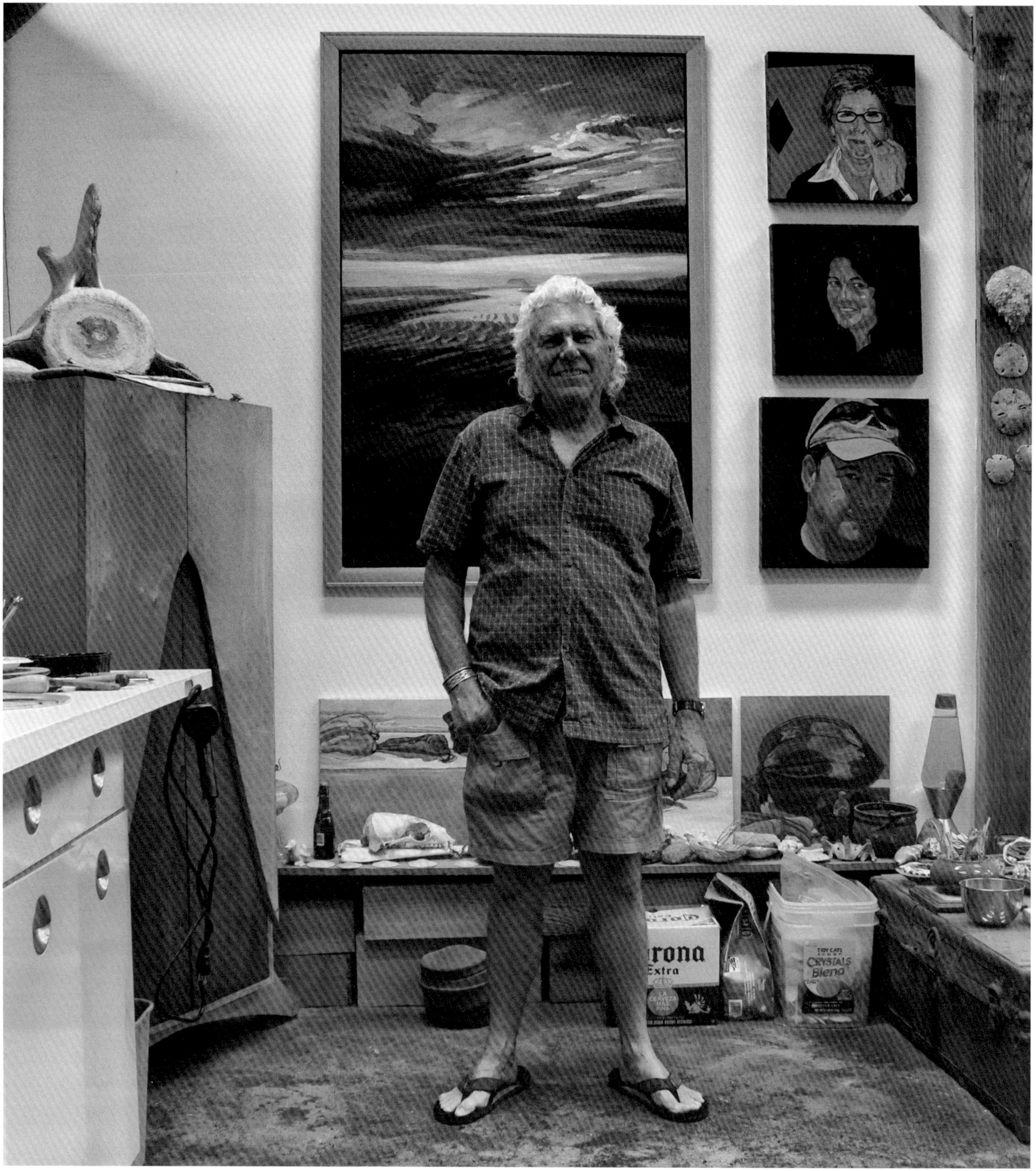
rona
Extra
TIDY CATS
CRYSTALS
Blend

Stuart Burton

April, 2015

I had been to Stuart's studio before, many years ago, but didn't recognize it when I first drove up. A much larger space than the charming, ramshackle garage of his COVA Open Studio days, this studio has abundant light. His studio serves also as a frame shop. Ever the prolific artist/teacher, Stuart continues to teach in downtown San Diego and travel to his place in Baja on weekends where he has another studio. Very relaxed in his studio, as he is in his own skin, Stuart exudes the confident painter and outdoors person he is. Paintings are everywhere that he works on them in groups, starting one here and moving on only to come back later and finish ones started earlier. I've noticed this is a practice of many painters. And, doing the same, I always thought I was weird.

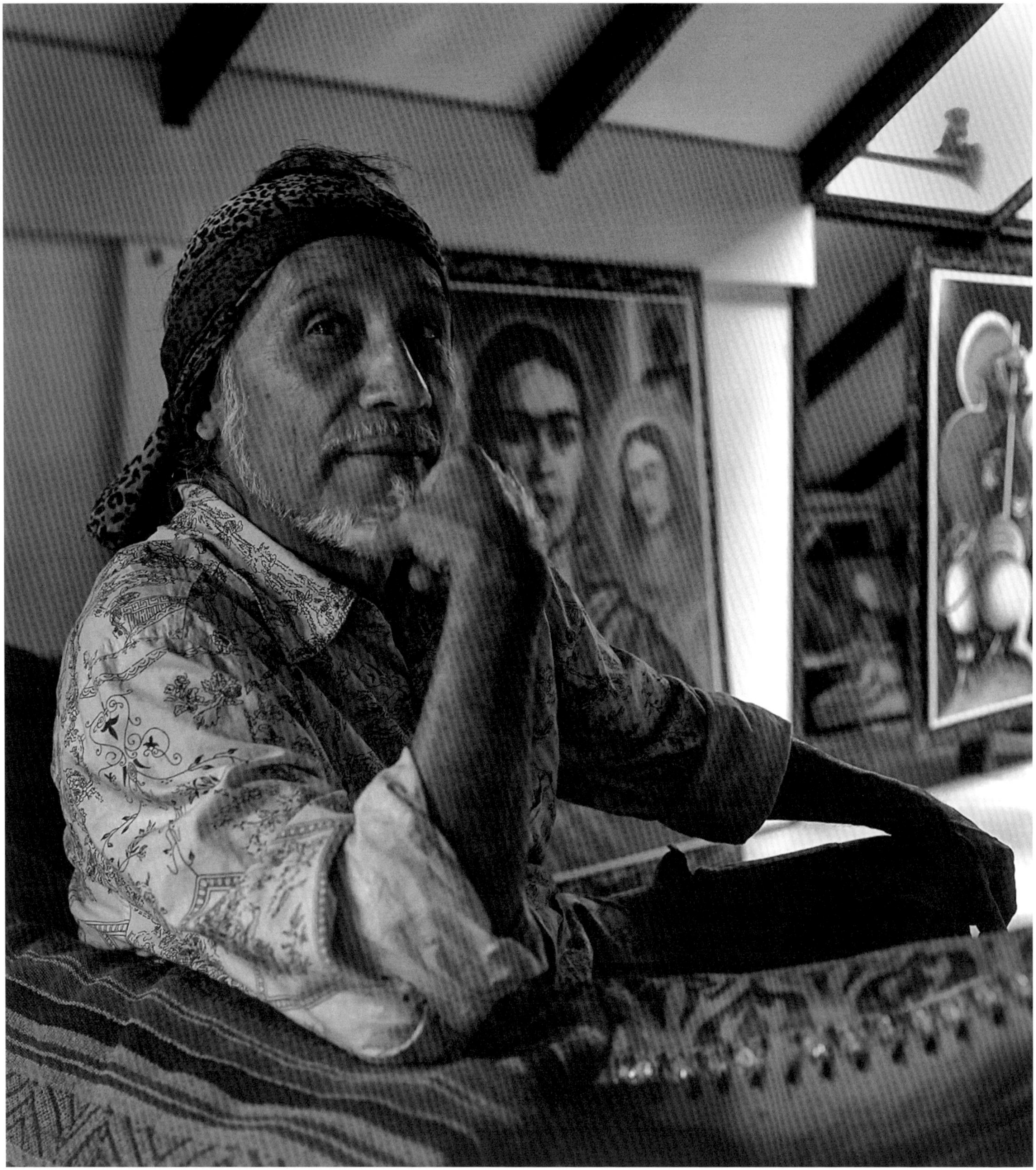

Mario Torero

May, 2015

In my years as executive director for COVA I had the opportunity to work with some of the artists in the Chicano community. I found them to be very passionate about their work and community and unabashedly outspoken politically. Mario was very much the activist artist in the Chicano community, specifically speaking out for the protection of the Chicano Park murals. His passion translates into his work. My challenge was to portray Mario in a more thoughtful moment as he argued his points.

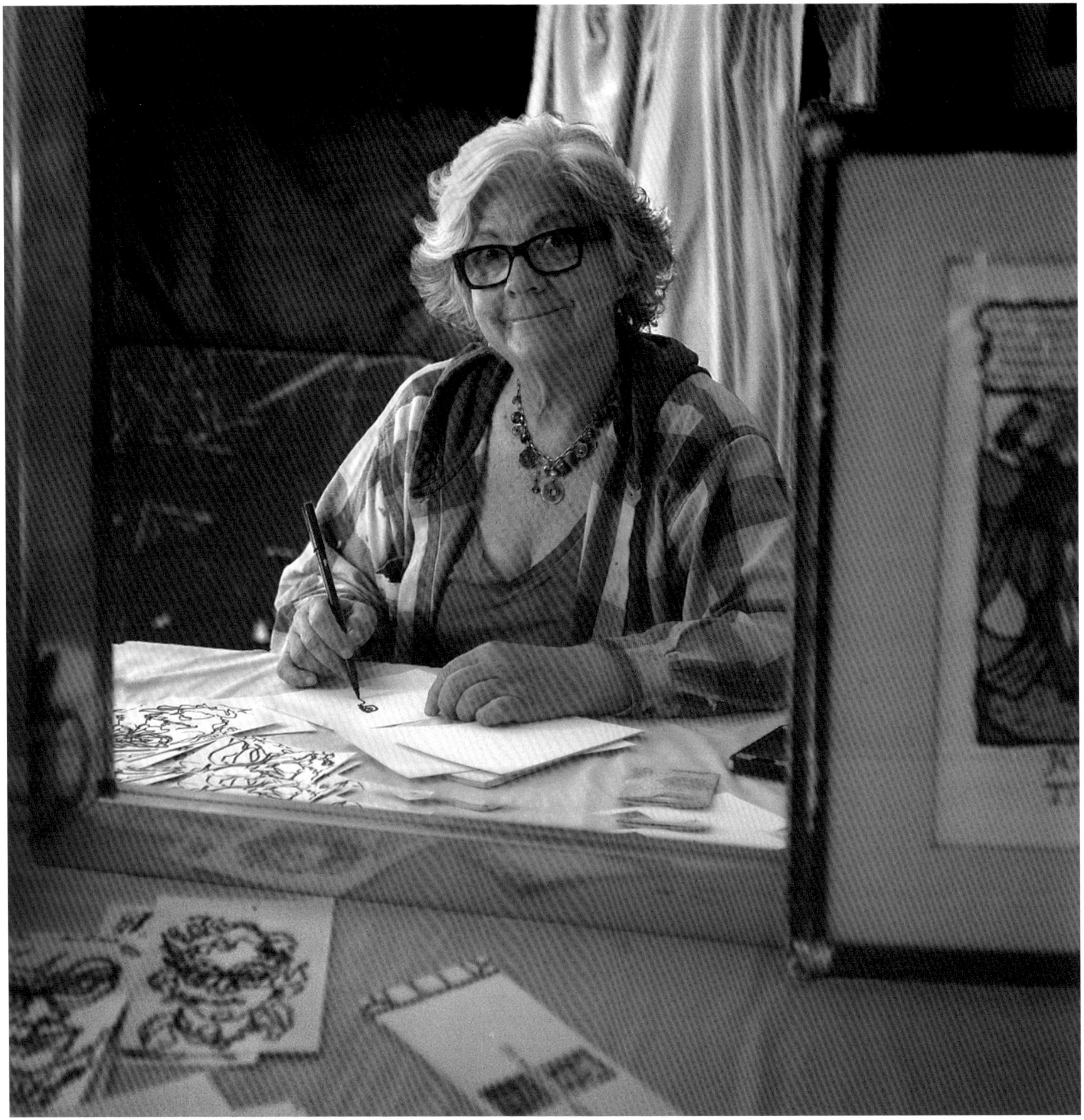

Cindy Zimmerman

June, 2015

Just coming off a stressful teaching session of five classes at three community colleges, I found Cindy trying to find her artist muse when I stepped into her studio. Ever the calm, well-spoken Cindy, who exudes warm Southern charm, she was most gracious in allowing me into her studio. We had not seen each other in some time and tried to decide when we first met in the art community. I allowed Cindy to find her comfort zone, as I've tried to do with most portrait subjects. She decided to start with a self-portrait series at the mirror, using her opposite hand. I'd seen some of her work before, influenced by comics and wondered how she arrived at her love of drawing.

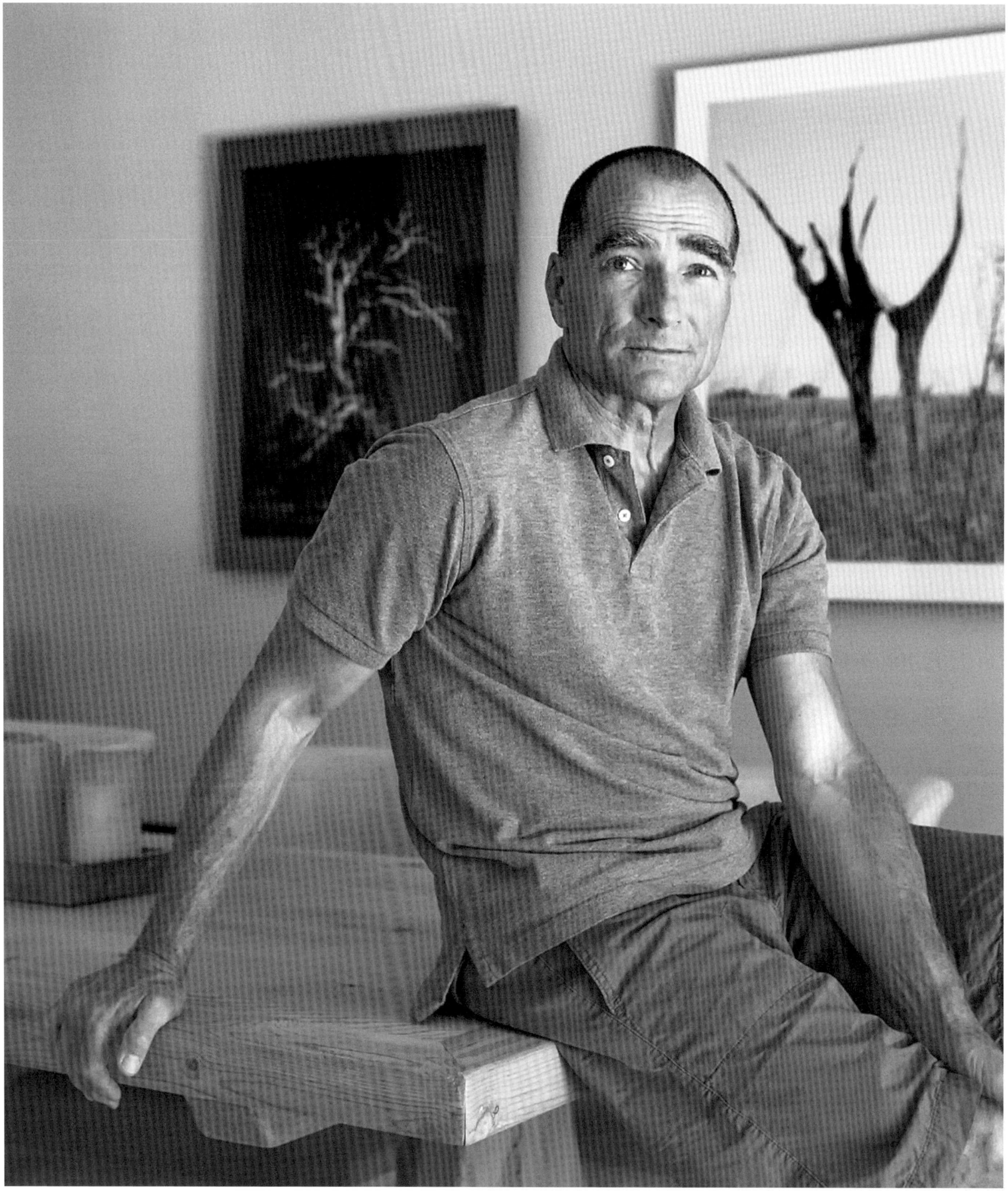

Philipp Scholz Rittermann

June, 2015

I've always looked up to Philipp, as I have to Suda House, both consummate photographers and instructors. Feeling a little intimidated, I found Philipp just as approachable as when I first met him many years ago. It put me at ease. Since then, he's gained more recognition and stature for his fine work. At the time of our portrait shoot, he was a bit preoccupied by his wife, who had been ill and needed to see a doctor. I offered to return at another date, but he said to go ahead. Since he informed me that his studio is really just computers and printers now, we set up the photo shoot in their beautiful home designed by his interior designer wife. Philipp of course had several of his photos hanging on walls. We talked a bit about how he grew up partly in the Canary Islands, and the travel that has influenced his work. Then I learned that Philipp got to assist Arnold Newman on a photo shoot in San Diego. Philipp had a number of interesting stories about Arnold and how he approached his portrait photography. Arnold Newman has been my muse throughout *The Artist Portrait Project*, so I was intrigued with Philipp's experience with Mr. Newman.

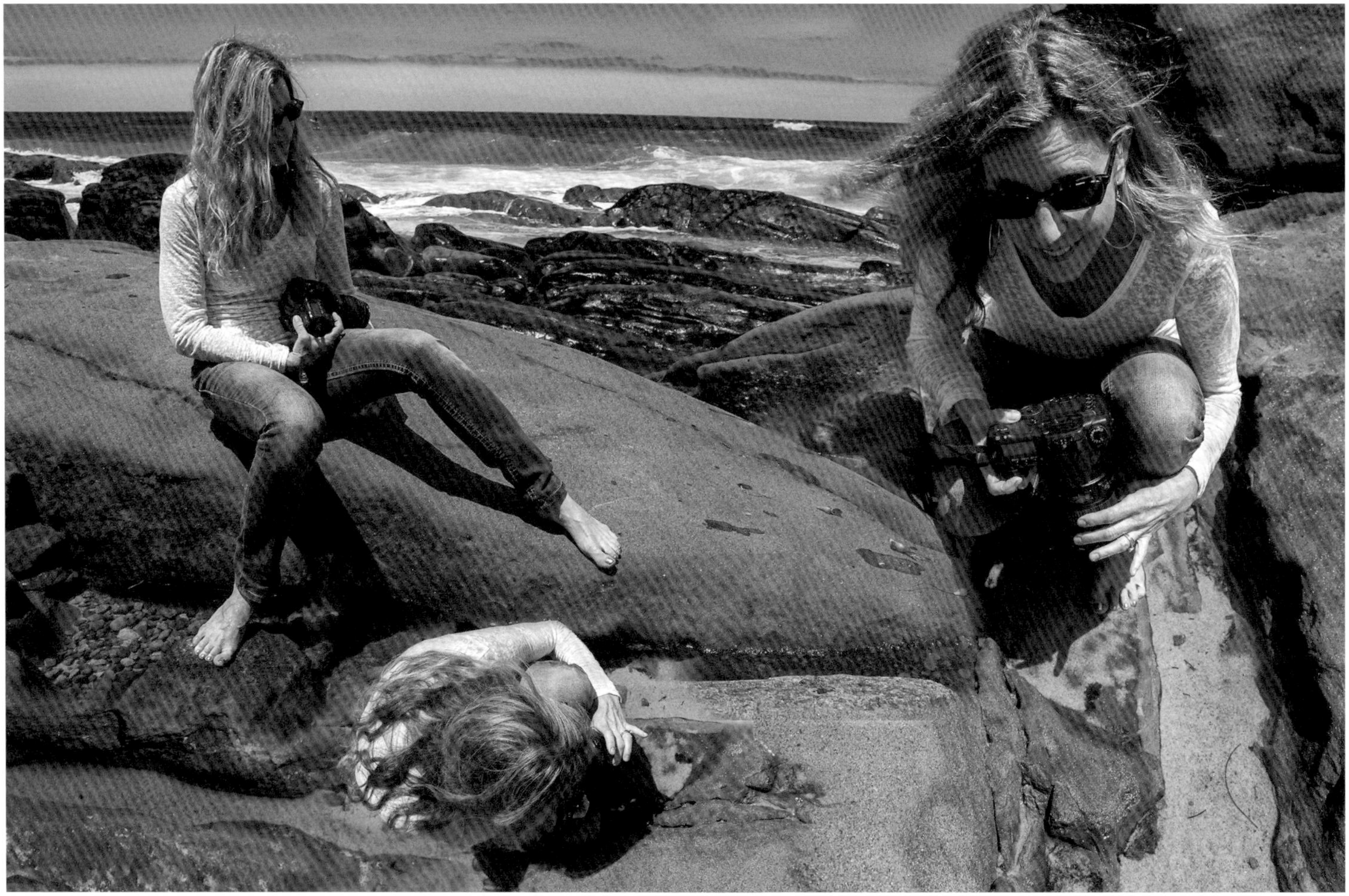

Dana Montlack

July, 2015

Dana has two studios, one here on the beach at Windansea, La Jolla, and the other in Atlanta, Georgia. She is working with a scientist she has been paired with at the Scripps Research Institute, on an environmental project examining climate change to be exhibited in 2017. Not having access to her at the research facility necessitated creating her portrait in the natural world, the focus of her project, at the beach. Due to the rough rocky beach terrain, I chose to photograph her working using my digital camera, not my large film camera. Her artist tool of choice is the digital camera, so it was fitting.

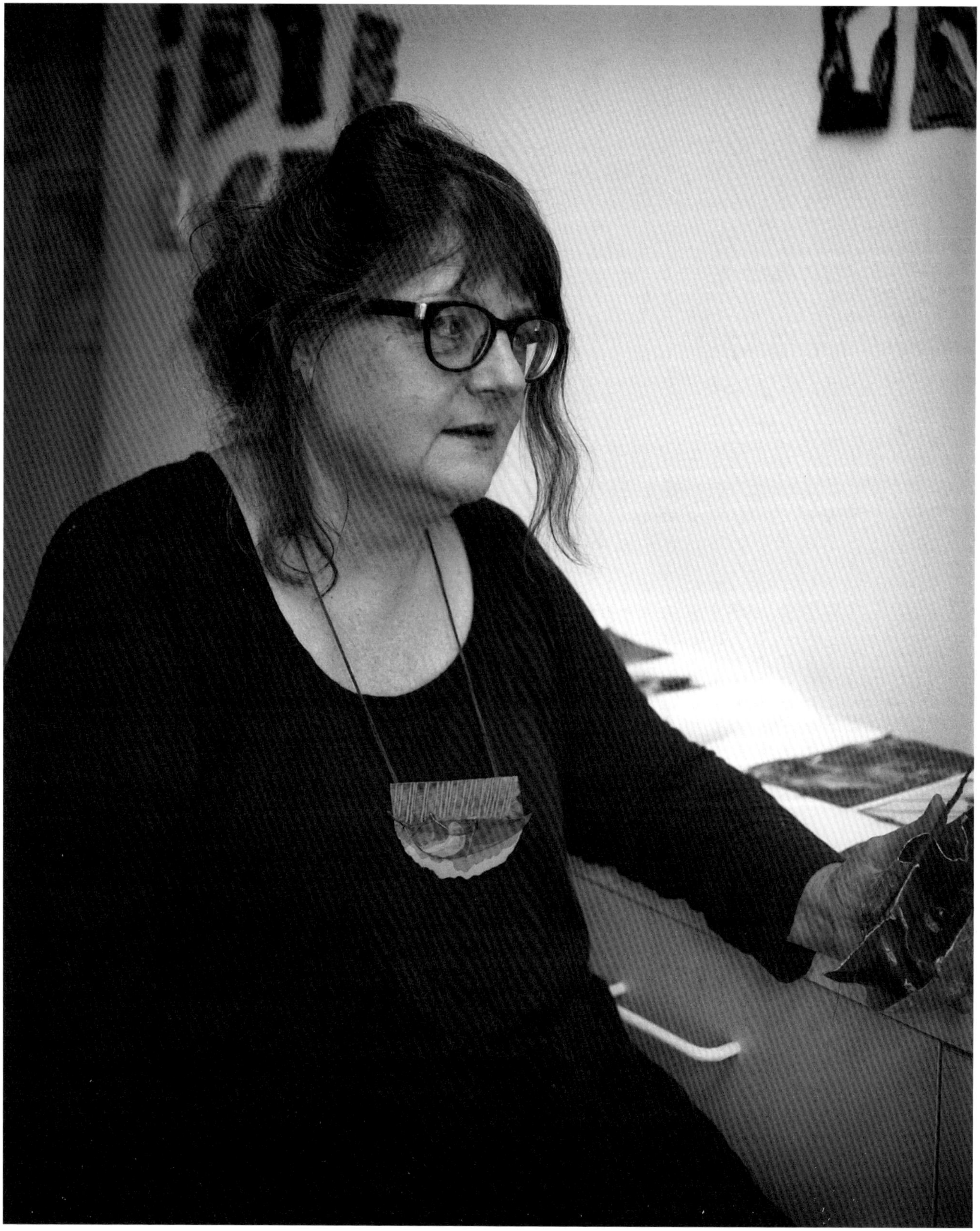

Georgia K. Laris

July, 2015

Georgia's home is her studio, although she kept telling me that her modified garage was the real deal. Georgia was somewhat relieved that I did not need to go into her "studio" after all and photographed her around her home where all of her art is displayed. She didn't even have to clean up her studio! You can see Georgia's design influence in each room. Though she has been teaching at Mesa College for many years and recently retired as the Art Department head, she has always managed to create work. I settled on two spaces for her portrait where the lighting was good. It was fun catching up while I proceeded to futz around with the camera. She then began to relax and look "arty," thinking about the next piece she needed to work on. Always working!

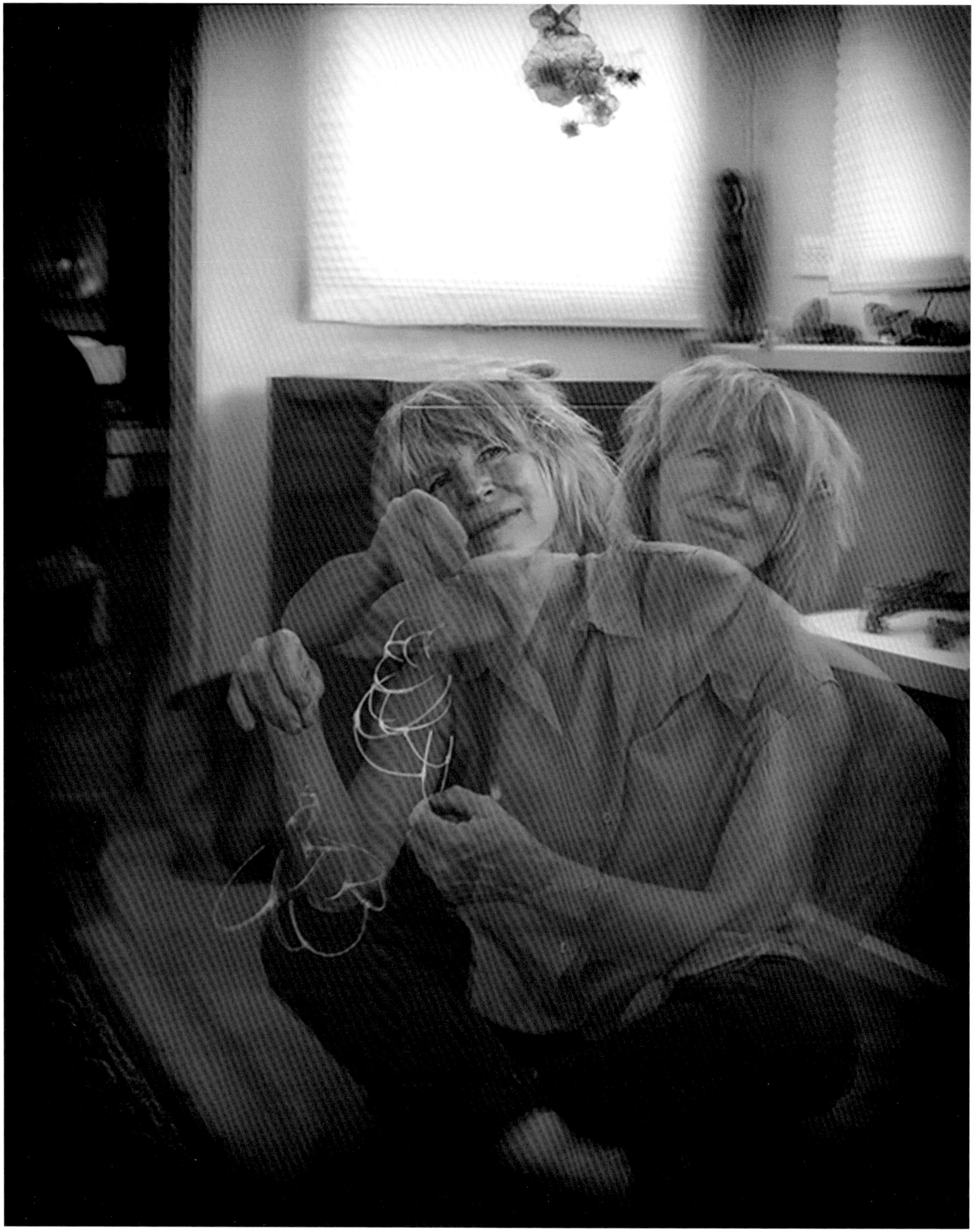

Anne Mudge

July, 2015

Somehow Anne and I got our wires crossed about our portrait appointment. I showed up. She was surprised. I left for an hour while she got ready and then came back. Then on to the portrait session. Anne and her husband live in a cozy mobile home in Fallbrook. She no longer had her studio since her last public art project ended. At first, she was somewhat concerned about that, but I reassured her that was not going to be a problem. After a brief look around the home, I decided on a particular corner that was well lit and had several of her pieces displayed. Since she'd just started working on a new model of a piece, I suggested that she hold it during the portrait session. That worked well because it allowed her to relax and think about her work . . . and not me with a camera. This resulted in a double exposure, as she nodded back and forth observing her model. It's always great to visit with Anne, but before we knew it, I was finished.

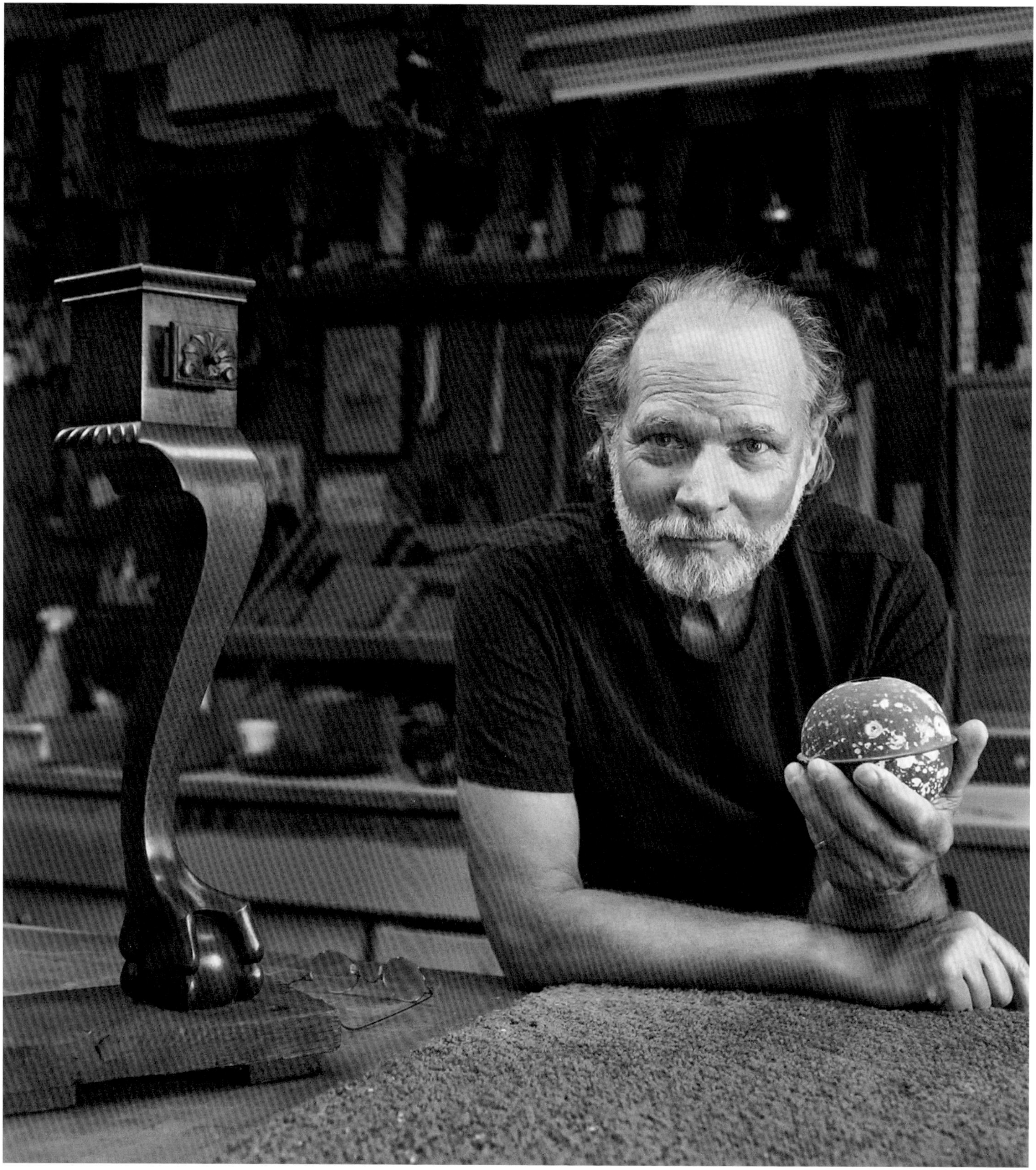

Paul Henry

August, 2015

Met up with Paul in his fine art furniture workshop in Carlsbad. He's had his studio since he first appeared in Open Studios many years ago. Instead of working with galleries, he now markets and sells his work from his website. The space was large and airy with a north-facing skylight, so lighting was not a challenge. Different spaces off the main workshop housed pieces that were quite intriguing, a cross between sculpture and fine art furniture. We selected a piece that perhaps demonstrates the less utilitarian aspect of his work that is both fun and beautiful. Having him situate himself with this piece on his worktable called for some other element . . . another round object he could hold. He looked a bit bemused at my request, but did come up with a metal ball on one of his shelves that worked. I wanted his bemusement of my project reflected in his portrait. Paul was very interested in my wooden field camera and took iPhone pictures of it. Maybe his next project will be to use this image in a new work.

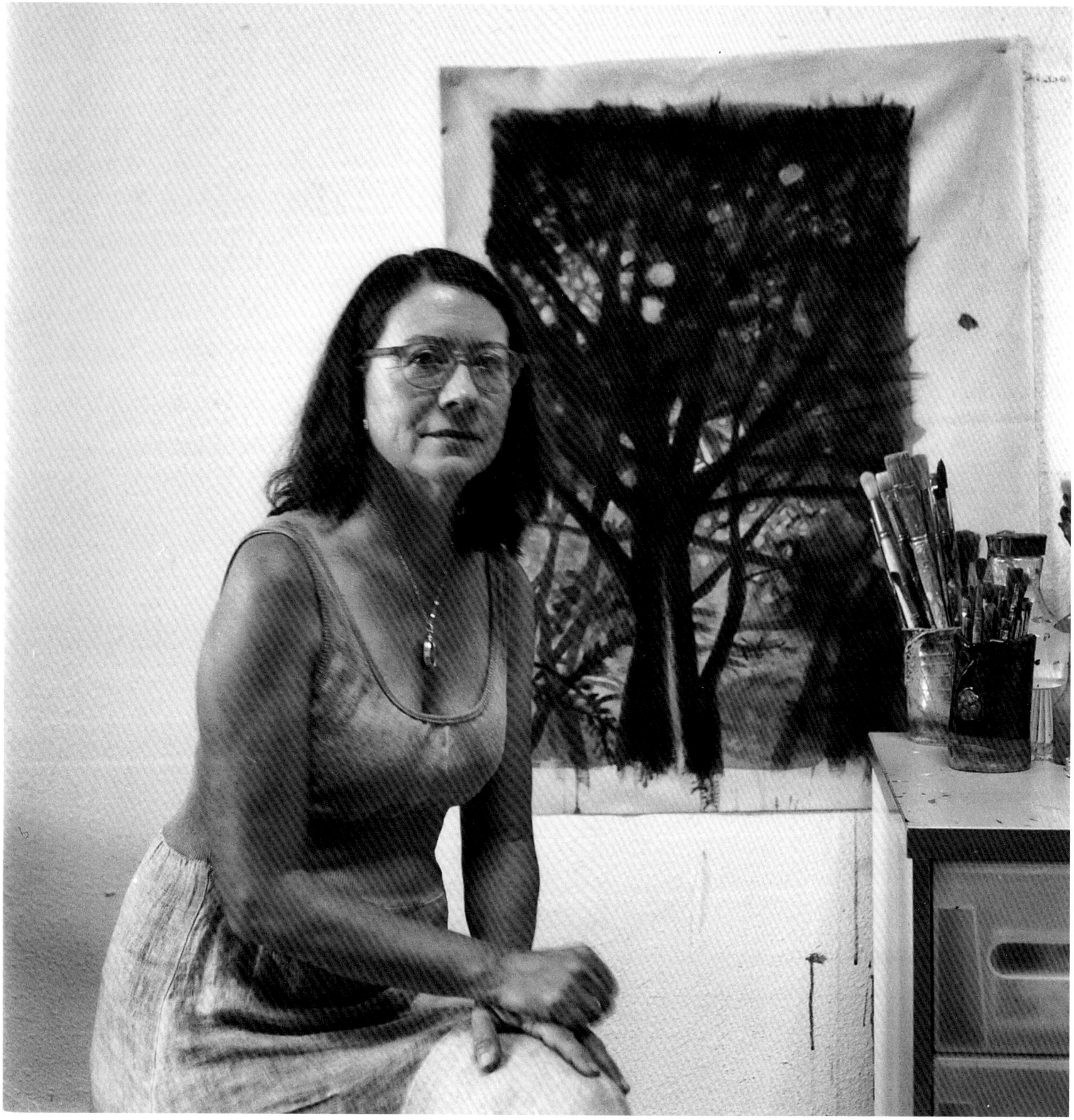

Grace Matthews

August, 2015

A hot Sunday morning for a portrait shoot could be a challenge, but Grace rose to the occasion and we settled on a couple of possibilities. The studio is a space shared with two other artists, The Three Graces Studio. It was evident that each artist's work had some influence on the others. It also became evident that Grace was used to posing for photos, and that was what I wanted to avoid. That was my challenge. I got her to talk a bit about the work she does with Faith Ringgold, a well-known multi-media artist famous for her quilted story telling. This worked because she no longer focused on me and the camera and began to relax.

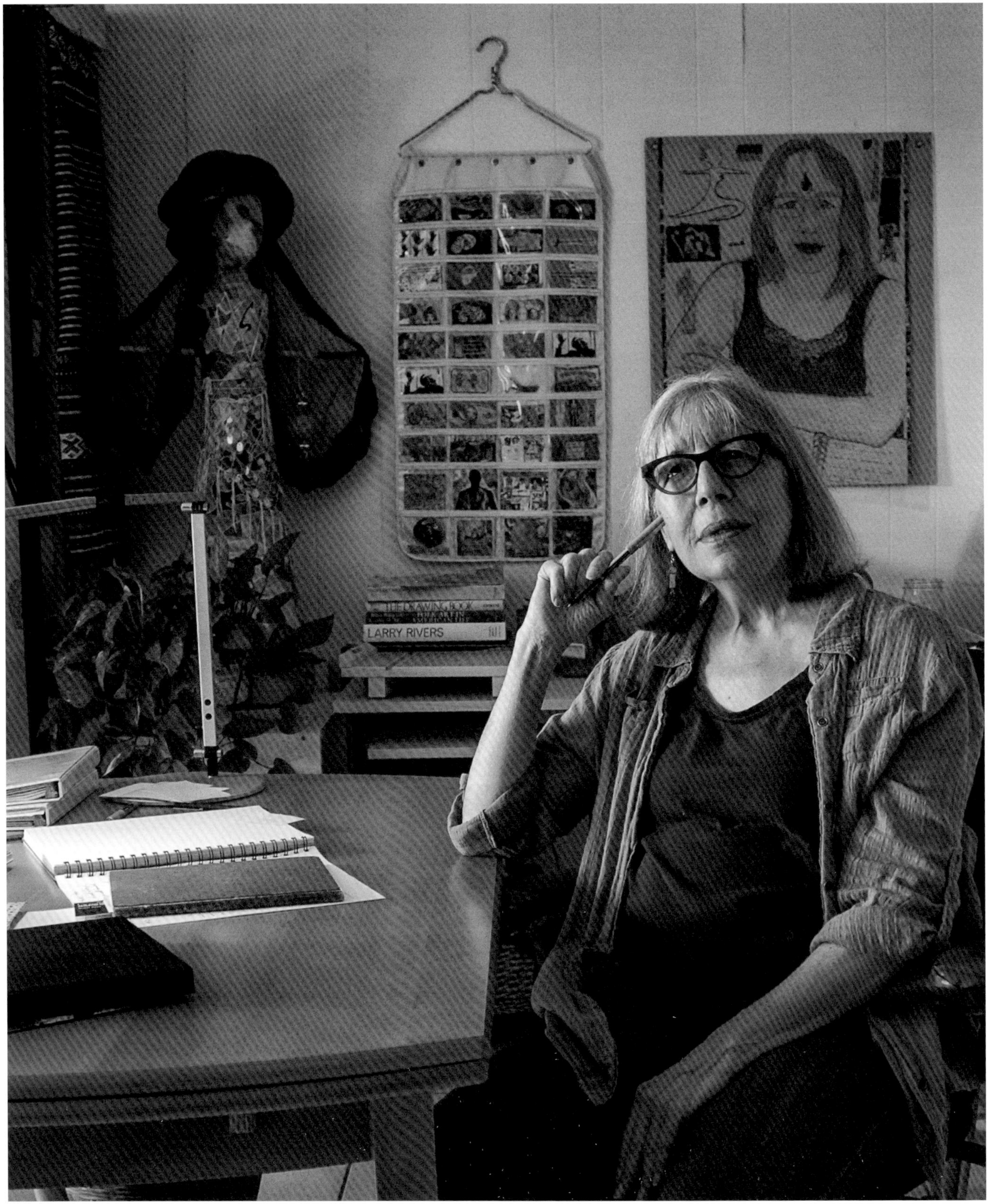
THE DRAWING BOOK
LARRY RIVERS

Diane Gage

April, 2016

Returning to my project after a hiatus of almost six months seemed a bit daunting. I chose to photograph Diane Gage, a poet and art collaborator, as my next subject for the project. Diane is the consummate conversationalist, warm and inviting and someone who can put a person at ease immediately. I've known Diane over the years, seeing her mostly at art openings and women's shows. In her own words, she is a "joiner" of art groups. I first became acquainted with Diane through the Women's Caucus, a group member of COVA. She has a reputation of collaborating with other artists in projects that focus on the word and image art, especially in book- making. Her home studio reflects that creative bent. Her home is her studio. You open the door and it's like walking into a book. Wherever you turn you see books, many created by her, as well as collaborative book projects. While there were many wonderful places in her home to photograph her, I wanted to focus on her thoughtfulness that she projected in her face and demeanor and work.

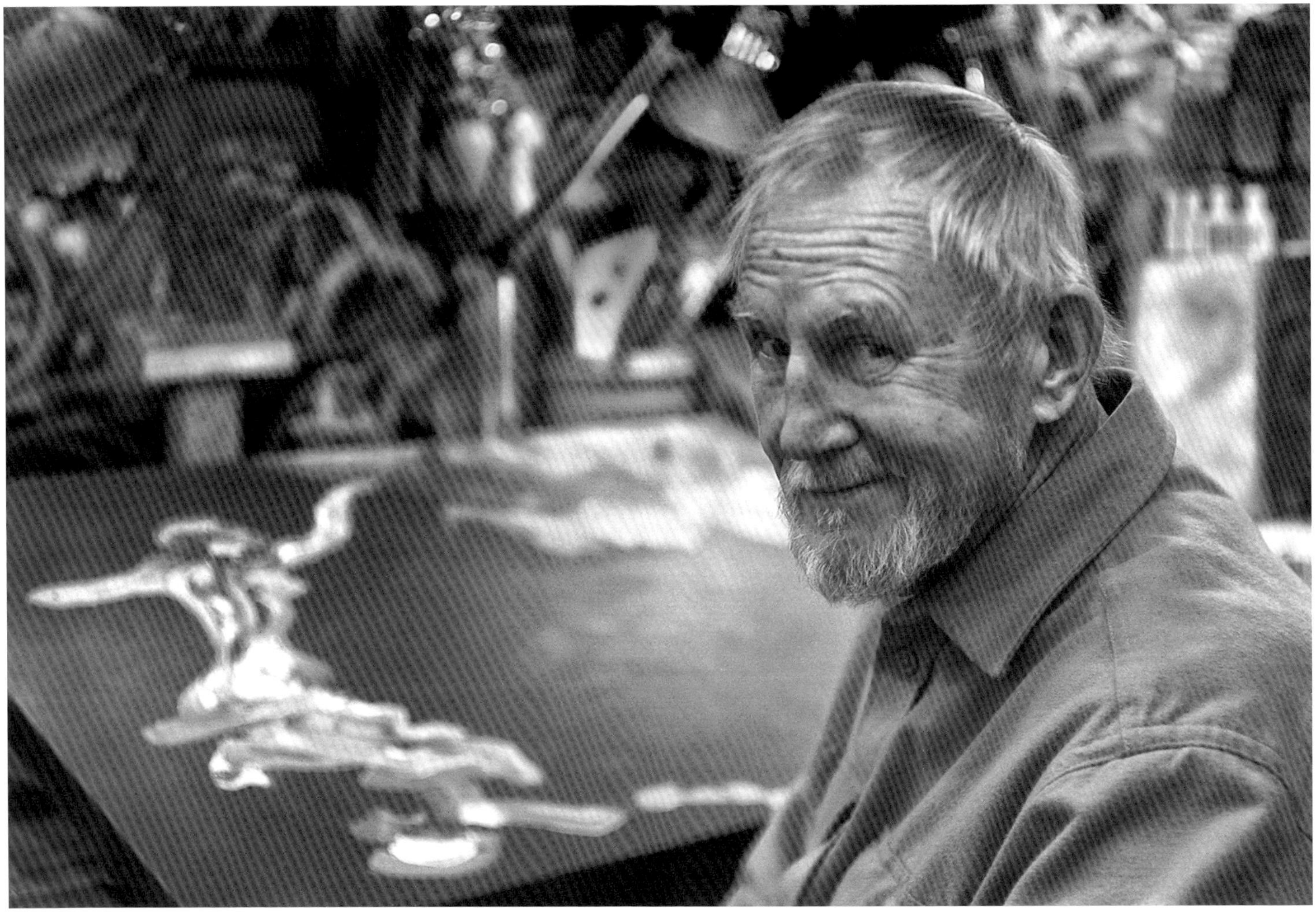

Joe Nyiri

May, 2016

I had not seen Joe in several years, like so many of the other artists in this project. Joe has been photographed numerous times over the years. In fact, in December of 2015, KPBS did a documentary on him in his studio. I reviewed this video before visiting his studio and noted that Joe has several different facial expressions that reflects who he is. A happy and inquisitive artist, he has been prolific in his work. Joe Niyri's studio reflects his eclectic source of materials that go into his work and inspire him to create. Like so many other artists, his studio is jammed not only with curious materials but also completed work ready for exhibition or sale. Joe's inquisitive and fun-loving nature is seen in his work.

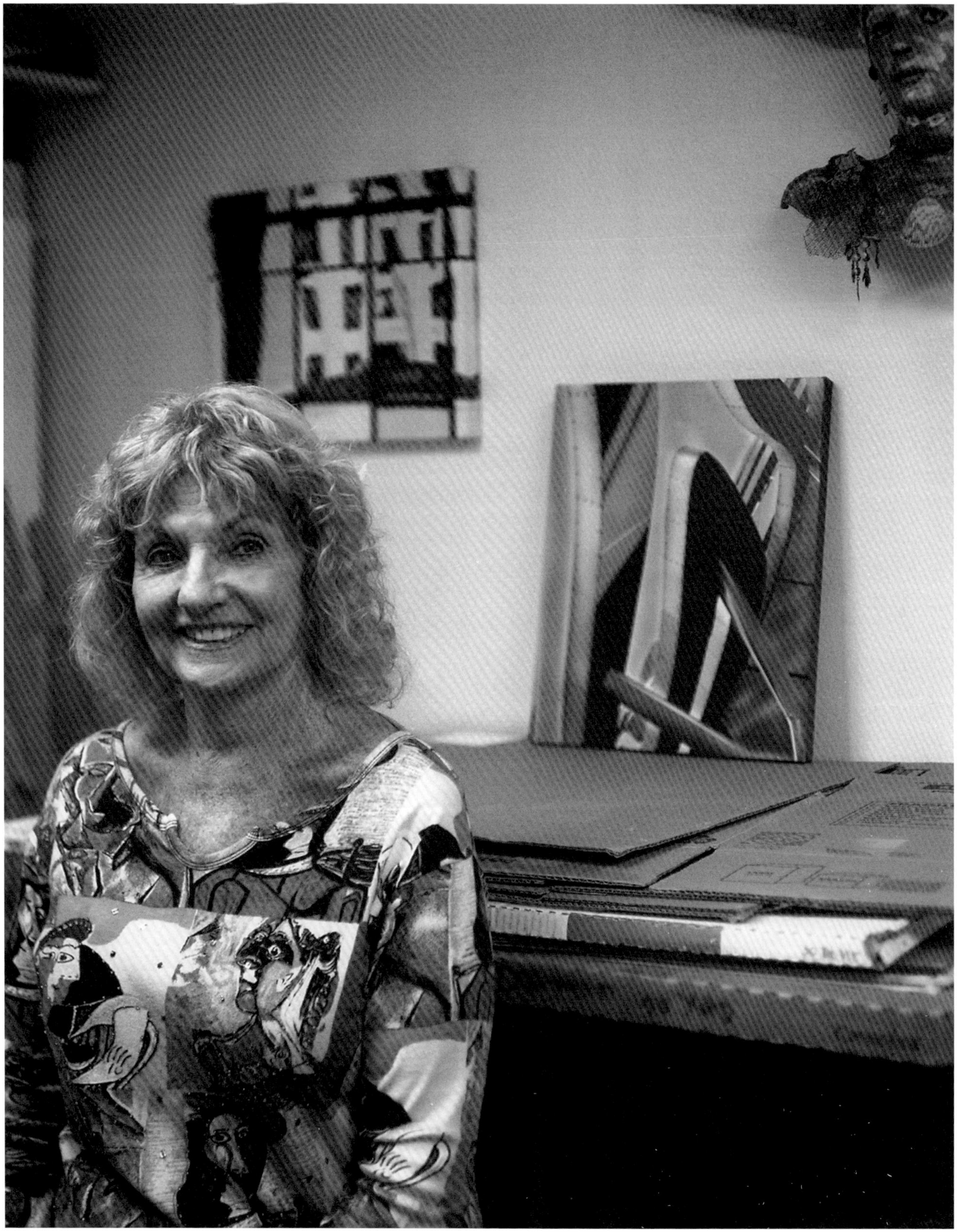

Pasha Turley

July, 2016

Pasha was my last portrait for the series.

As I proceeded through the project, I began to notice that I was selecting artists who were often also teachers at community colleges and universities. In fact, this realization became the impetus for the book and the reason I selected the artists I did. There are so many wonderful artists in San Diego, it was very difficult to make selections. In reality, the availability of the artist and their generous willingness to participate also became criteria for selection. Pasha was no exception. As an artist and teacher, her generous spirit prevails in all she does. She was always a busy lady. Occasionally we'd run into each other at openings and catch up a bit.

I'd tried a few times to connect with Pasha over a year. Unfortunately, she was in the midst of a life change, retirement and moving, so her availability became a challenge. I'd known Pasha through one of the group members of COVA, the Women's Caucus. At the time, I was ED of COVA, I'd not had the pleasure of really getting to know her. Not until we finally coordinated the portrait shoot did I begin to understand what challenges Pasha has had in her life and art. Through it all she has maintained a giving spirit that is reflected in her work.

Epilogue

In Celebration of My Fellow Artists of San Diego: Why photograph artists?

For thirteen years, I was the ED for COVA, Combined Organizations for the Visual Arts. My community was that of artists. In my daily responsibilities to the organization, I had the opportunity to meet many fellow artists who were trying to make a name and place for themselves in the art world. Over time, many of the artists became friends. Retiring and returning to school short-circuited my usual attendance at art openings and other art gatherings. Though I'd already begun *The Artist Portrait Project*, I found myself drifting further away from the everyday existence of my fellow creative artists. In the beginning, some ten years ago, I was enthused about meeting up with my artist friends and taking my 4x5 camera into their studios to capture them in their environment. About the same time, I lost my downtown studio to the development of the ballpark. The high ceilings and open space I was used to for painting was no longer available.

A confluence of events propelled me into the project. I moved my studio home, where it became relegated to the family room. Not only was it a lonelier existence, I also found the environment no longer conducive to painting. Hence, I moved toward photography when I returned to school. To keep in touch with my fellow artists, I found it beneficial to start *The Artist Portrait Project* as an entree into their studio lives. It was the most natural thing for me to do.

The Artist Portrait Project opened my eyes to seeing my fellow artists in a different light. Initially, my artist portraits tried to capture what I'd subconsciously observed for many years but had not put into words or images.

The work of many of my fellow artists very often reflected much about themselves personally, both in content and appearance. One might think it would be obvious that the artist's work would be an expression of who they were and their view of the world. This is the essence I have been challenged to capture in my portraits of San Diego artists. The artists chosen for the project came from different sources, and most are artists I've known and respected for many years. Some have been selected because they participated in the COVA Open Studios program or other COVA programs and exhibitions. All are artists I've known, some better than others.

I've admired all their work and thus they have had some impact on me as an artist. These are artists who have contributed to the creative culture of the region. It's not just about their work . . . it's about who they are, the creators of the fabric of culture in San Diego County.

The above is a statement of my original premise. This project is also about the persistence of the creative spirit.

What I discovered in the process of *The Artist Portrait Project* was more revealing about the artist culture of San Diego County than I'd anticipated. It has always fascinated me how my fellow artists can continue to do the work they do over time, under financial burdens and family responsibilities that would have stopped most people. Their creative spirit has been so strong that, in the light of economic struggles, many have found ways to support their need to create art. Many have become teachers, instructors, art school managers and some just got lucky and found financial support in other ways.

The book is dedicated to those who've continued to honor their own creative spirit and to those who've passed on that love of art and the artistic process to their students through community colleges, universities, and art schools. To those who've nurtured the creative spirit in others . . . I salute you!

Acknowledgments

Special thanks to my teachers, Professors Suda House and Jim Noel, who provided the inspiration for this endeavor.

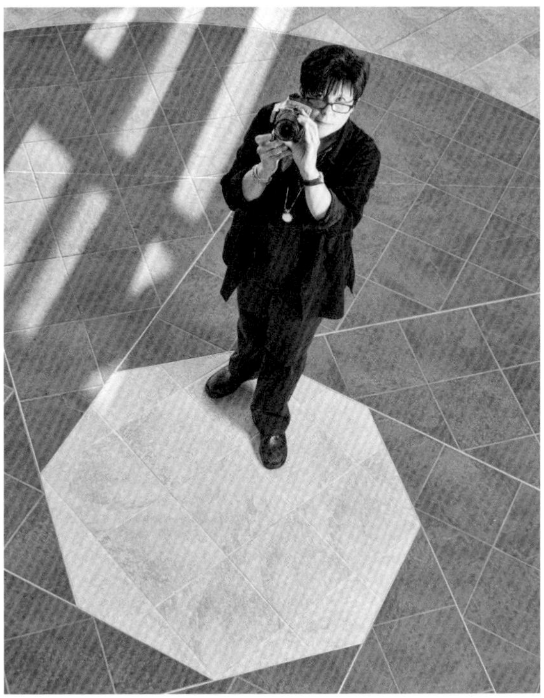

Suda House photo © William Gullett Photographer

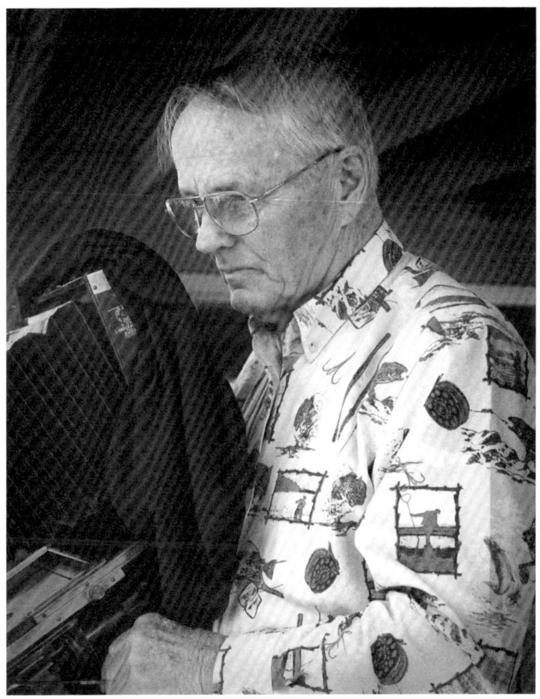

Jim Noel photo © Jennifer G. Spencer

My friend, artist's agent, and able copy editor, Claire Slattery.

Thanks to all of the artists who participated in this project and helped with their encouragement.

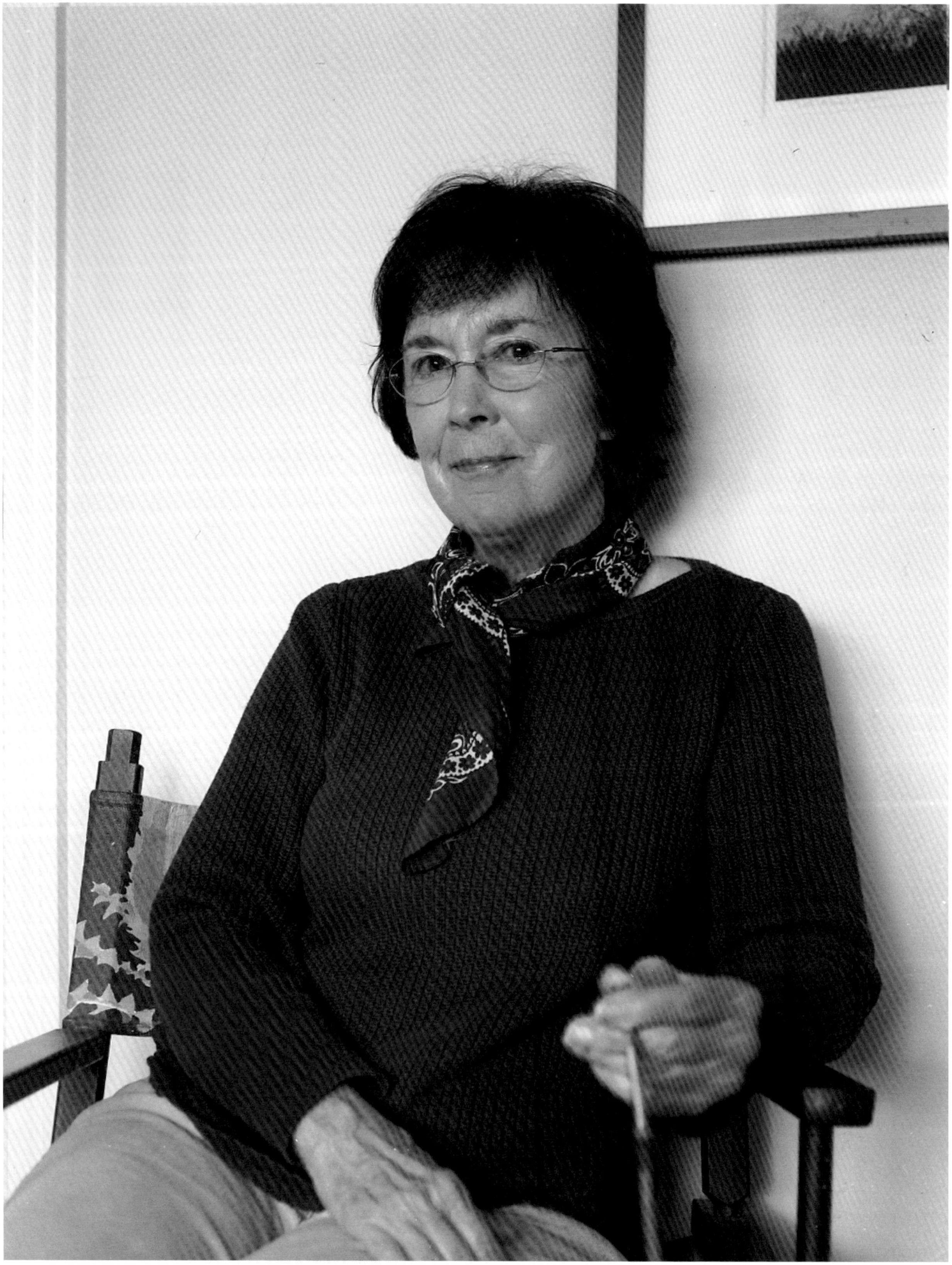

About the Author

Jennifer G. Spencer

Jennifer G. Spencer is a painter/photographer who creates images using alternative photographic processes and digital imagery. Jennifer's painting experience has informed her photography and the way she looks at the photographic image.

Jennifer's career began as a painter back east, in Massachusetts. After moving to California in the mid 1970s, her painting began to change. It was during her brief business adventure in painting backdrops for photographers that her interest in photography emerged. Jennifer's curiosity and creative interests blossomed after attending Grossmont Community College, where she acquired an Associate's Degree in Digital Art Media and Fine Art Photography. Jennifer began focusing on portraiture after leaving her job as executive director of visual arts organization at Combined Organizations for the Visual Arts.